THE IT FACTOR
Mindset of an Entrepreneur

The IT Factor: Mindset of an Entrepreneur
Copyright © 2017 Billy Kounoupis
Published by Star City Publishing

All rights reserved. No part of this book may be reproduced (except for inclusion in reviews), disseminated or utilized in any form or by any means, electronic or mechanical, including photocopying, recording, or in any information storage and retrieval system, or the Internet/World Wide Web without written permission from the author or publisher.

For further information, contact the author at:
Billy@allamericanhospitalitygroup.com
Tel: 610.419.2517

All American Hospitality Group
8 East Broad Street
2nd Floor
Bethlehem PA 18018

www.billysdiner.com
Printed in the United States

The IT Factor: Mindset of an Entrepreneur
Billy Kounoupis

1. Title 2. Author 3. Business

Library of Congress Control Number: : 2017901910
ISBN 13: 9780978958916

THE IT FACTOR
Mindset of an Entrepreneur

BILLY KOUNOUPIS

This book is dedicated to God, who has been good to me. With love and affection to my mother, Georgia Kounoupis, who sacrificed everything to give me everything. Your prayers, love, and belief in me taught me, "Yes, I can."

To my father and my hero, Pete Kounoupis, who continues to inspire me to live life with courage and no excuses, and my brother, George Kounoupis, whom I miss and wished we could have shared memories. They will live in my memory forever.

And to my wife, Yanna, who I love and adore as well as have the privilege to have as my partner in love, life, and business since 1999. Without you my dreams would have been nightmares. And to my amazing children, Panayioti, Georgia, and Michael, who bless my life with joy and happiness.

Contents

Preface 1

Introduction 5

Chapter One 17

Chapter Two 35

Chapter Three 47

Chapter Four 57

Chapter Five 65

Chapter Six 71

Chapter Seven 83

Chapter Eight 85

Chapter Nine 93

Chapter Ten 101

Acknowledgments 103

About the Author 107

Preface
Screwed

Typically when you see a preface, it's written by someone other than the author, but this is just the first of many unconventional things I'm going to do with this book. I have many wonderful people in my life who would have loved to write this preface, and would have done a great job, too, but I opted not to choose any of them because I wanted this book to be an honest, transparent representation of my perspective from start to finish.

"Then why have a preface at all?" you might wonder. Well I'll tell you, it's because I have a few things about myself and where I came from that I wanted to put out there before you start on your path—and frankly, I just couldn't find a place to put this stuff. So here it is.

Many times in my life people have seen me smile, but trust me, I wasn't always smiling from the inside out. Rather, I was *rotting* from the inside out. One time in particular was when my failures in business combined with the demise of my relationships with a few aunts, uncles, and cousins. Circumstances led me to feel abandoned by these otherwise close members of my family, and I felt like I could no longer trust anyone. My father and brother had passed away, and if not for my mother, I would have been totally alone. My love and respect for her forced me to put on a façade to protect her. She was widowed and had lost her oldest son, and I didn't want to cause her any more pain.

So I shut down; I didn't want to communicate with anyone. I was content suppressing my misery to a point of numbness, both mentally and physically. I was nobody, going nowhere, and I didn't care. My anger had peaked to a point where my only emotions were negative, and logic ceased to exist. My failure made me hopeless, careless, and godless. People that I had thought cared for me wound up mocking and ridiculing me. I felt betrayed by friends, family, and God.

My mother was concerned about well-being, of course. She was so concerned, in fact, that she booked a ticket for me to Greece to calm down and think things through. She owned a little apartment in Athens, and thought the best thing would be for me to get away from all the negativity and go to a place where I knew no one, and no one knew about me or my business failures—a place where I could hopefully find peace. She knew I didn't want to listen to advice from anyone and had to let my anger run its course.

Prior to that trip, all my mom could do was pray. She would have our priest, Father Nicholas, visit me almost weekly at our apartment (and in fact, he still does this today). He would bring holy bread to our home and speak with me. He was always calm and mild-mannered regardless of my state. He never challenged me, but shared his thoughts of wisdom and sincere love. He was so kind and caring, and would always say something motivational and spiritual to help stir some positivity in my life. One quote I still remember to this day was when he said, "Watch your steps. Think it through. If you're careless, even your own teeth will bite your tongue." With this message, he tried to tell me to be careful or I would build a life of regret.

No matter how great his advice was at the time, all I heard was, "Blah blah blah." My mind, body, and spirit were dark. I didn't want love or lectures. I was approaching a point of no return. To quote a line I think I heard from a movie, if I'd had a guardian angel, he would've said, "I'm going to lose my job and wind up in hell with this asshole."

Failure in everything, combined with the vitriol and lies of people you love and trust—this can be a toxic concoction. But this is life. It's an emotional roller coaster. Thankfully, my mom knew I had to be removed from everything negative. She didn't want me to hide my fears. She wanted me to face them, but on *my* terms. It sucked leaving the only person that I trusted and loved, and I knew it was even worse for my mom having to send her only son away.

On the day of my departure, Father Nicholas said a prayer and gave me a bit of wisdom. "Never lie to someone you trust," he said, "and don't trust someone who lies to you. You can count on God, so place your trust in Him."

With this thought in my heart, I went away for almost a year. In Greece, I worked as a bartender and waiter, a harsh reminder of the failures I had left back home. Life was tough for me, given that my Greek was terrible and my communication skills not the greatest even on a good day. But I didn't have to share my failures, and that made me happy.

Then the strangest thing happened: I got angry with myself. I hadn't acknowledged my failure, and I hadn't faced reality. I was living in a bubble of bullshit. It was then that I knew: The time had come for me to go back home. I realized that the mental beating I had given myself for over a year had been so brutal that I could deal with anyone and anything. I had hit the bottom, and my only way was up. Nothing was going to stop me.

From that day forward, I welcomed every obstacle and every challenge. If I couldn't open the door, I was going to break it open. The only person who could stop me was God, and God was on my side.

Why do I bring this up? Why did I choose to start this book with thoughts on the worst period of my life? Simple. This story illustrates the great struggle that comes with accepting a new mindset. It took losing a business and the relationships with many of my family and friends for me to realize that my first mindset wasn't going to get me anywhere. Then it took a year waiting tables in Greece for me to realize that a new mindset would dig me out of the hole I found myself in. As you engage with the chapters to come, you're likely to face your share of doubt and negativity as well. When that happens, it's important to remember to trust *yourself* and not your negativity, as I once learned the hard way. Ultimately, even if you can hear your friends and family doubting or ridiculing the dreams I know you're going to follow, you and God are the only people you need on your side.

Introduction
The Pain Is What Drives Us

Let's start on a light and fluffy note, shall we? There's no easy way to say this, but it's a grim job market out there. One of the reasons it's so tough to find work is because companies are still downsizing even as the economy supposedly recovers from one of the worst recessions in history. Call it a shifting economic climate. Call it a new world order for the way business is done. Call it bad management. Whatever you want to call it, it seems like companies that have been around for a lifetime are now in the process of closing their doors.

Macy's, for instance, recently announced a plan to shut down over forty stores. Dunkin Donuts will be closing one hundred locations. Even McDonald's, that bastion of fast food growth, will shutter up over seven hundred locations in the coming months. It's starting to look like the only people hiring are Walmart and maybe a few drug cartels.

But enough of this! This is not the time for gloom and doom. I'm writing this book because, believe it or not, I do have something real to tell you—something meaningful that will make a difference in your life. And that something real and meaningful is this: as entrepreneurs, the *pain* is what drives us.

Okay, okay. You're thinking, *He said we were going to quit with the doom and gloom.* Fair enough. We're going to get more positive here, I promise. When I write the word "pain," I don't mean to use it in a negative light. Sure, pain is pain. Nobody *wants* it. But if we're talking about entrepreneurial pursuits, as long as you know how to use pain to your advantage, it *always* leads to positive change. We're living through painful times right now. Let's harness that pain for positive change.

Now you might ask yourself, "What qualifies Billy Kounoupis to write about *any* topic, let alone the one about the entrepreneurial mindset?" If you read my first book, you know that it's an apt question. I didn't graduate high school with the highest of marks. And I didn't graduate college. I mean, what did I need an education for anyway? So I could compete with college dropouts like Bill Gates, Steve Jobs, and Mark Zuckerberg? Only kidding. The fact is, I'm qualified to speak on the subject of entrepreneurship not because of my education, but because of my *failures*.

Since we're bonding now, please allow me to share with you the events that completely changed my life. First, when I was six, my brother died in my arms. At the time, I didn't know he was sick—that he had leukemia. We were playing a game of tag, and the moment I tagged him, he fell to the ground. He died right there with a six-year-old me by his side.

The rest of my childhood was perfectly idyllic. But then, nine years later, when I was fifteen, tragedy would strike again. Back then, I would walk to my parents' diner every day after school. My mom, Georgia, and my dad, Pete, were workaholics, so I was surprised to arrive at the diner one day to find that neither of them was there. I asked some of the employees on duty if they had seen my parents, and none of them seemed to want to give me a straight answer. I knew something was up, but I couldn't put my finger on it until the phone rang. It was a nurse, and she asked me to get to the hospital as quick as I could.

When I arrived, I immediately rushed to my dad's room. I couldn't control my tears at the sight of him. He didn't look like the man I had grown to love and admire. He looked like a hollowed-out version of that man.

"Why are you crying?" my dad asked with a smile.

I told him that I was scared and that I didn't think I could live without him.

"Don't be scared," he told me, "of *anything*." Then he looked me straight in the eyes and said, "You live every day, and you die once."

He went on to remind me that I would be okay because I lived in a country of endless possibilities. "You have so many more opportunities than I ever had," he said. At the time, I had no clue what he was talking about, but now that I'm older and wiser, I get it. My dad was so right. I had a hundred times more opportunity to succeed than he ever did. First, I was born and raised in the best country in the world, the United States of America—a country that embraces entrepreneurship. My father, meanwhile, had left the old country with only $20 in his pocket. I had everything and he had nothing.

Actually, that's not true. At least not entirely. He had an entrepreneurial spirit and the ambition and desire to stake his claim in the world and succeed. My father, God rest his soul, used to say that he would eat, sleep, and drink the same way whether he had $1 in his pocket or $1 million in his bank account. Here's why: he started his life with almost nothing. During World War II, processed food was nonexistent, at least in Sparta. Everyone farmed back then. They lived off the land. When the crops were bountiful, Spartans would harvest olives from their olive trees, get eggs from their chickens, pick vegetables from their gardens, and so on. At the time, though, the country suffered from a widespread food shortage, in part because the crops were drying up and in part because Greece was under invasion by the Nazis. This meant that to eat was not a right but a privilege. Waste was unheard of.

My grandfather died while my father was young, so that left my grandmother to care for her children alone. All of this left her extremely poor, but she didn't want to appear that way to the rest of the community. She didn't want people looking down their noses at her about her lack of funds or her quality as a parent. So even when she didn't have enough food to feed her six kids, she would set out a big pot on the fire for all to see. Every time someone came by to ask what she had in the pot, she would describe a grand stew she had planned for the children. Everyone would be appropriately impressed. The trouble was that the pot never had anything more than water in it.

"When will the stew be ready?" her children would ask her all day.

"Soon," she would always say—and there was never any answer but "soon."

She would keep the water boiling right up until her children fell asleep. In this way, my father went to bed hungry many nights as a kid.

The IT Factor

For a mother, there's nothing worse than wanting to feed your child and not being able to. For a child, there's nothing worse than seeing your mother struggling and wanting to tell her that you don't want to be a burden, even though you're hungry. That's what drove my father toward the entrepreneurial mindset we'll be discussing in this book. That pain of seeing no food, no job, no money—of living in a country under the invasion of the Nazis—was the driving force that made my dad want a better life for himself and for his family. He wasn't just an entrepreneur in the sense that he wanted to create a job for himself; he was an entrepreneur in the sense that he was passionate about his family and freedom and hard work, and he was willing to do whatever it took to improve his life.

That's when my dad started looking abroad. He knew he needed to get out of Greece and go to a country where, even if he didn't know anyone or was able to speak the language, he would at least have the freedom to learn everything he needed to on his own. Naturally, that country turned out to be the United States.

Like many immigrants from his generation, he came through Ellis Island. He spent those first few nights at the bus terminal. It might as well have been a five-star hotel by the standards of his village back in Greece. My father was determined to make a better life in the US, so he quickly found a job working as a dishwasher in a restaurant. I remember him telling me how thrilled he was to have that job because he finally had access to some food and a paycheck. Also, this job provided him with his first opportunity to learn a trade that would come to shape his life. From his dishwashing station, he would watch the cooks picking up new insights about the craft of cooking every day. "Your eyes need to steal," he often told me as I was growing up. That's the literal translation from the Greek, anyway. What he meant was that you learn more by watching than by talking.

While he stole with his eyes, he would also pick up snippets of conversation from the cooks and servers, and would eventually piece them together into a rough command of English that he blended with Greek. "Grenglish" we called it.

Eventually Dad got settled in to a routine that allowed him enough money to send back to the old country to help out his brothers and sisters. Then one day, he received news from my grandmother that my mom was working in a factory in Canada. Now I don't mean to put my mom on the spot, but rumor had it that my dad had a crush on her back in Greece. Obviously he never said anything to anyone at the time. And anyway, with his lack of education, job, or money, it's not like he would have made for the ideal prince charming before he made his way in the States. To be honest, now that I write about the situation, I understand completely why my father-in-law looked at me the way he did when I started to date his daughter.

Well, love is a funny thing. My father learned where my mother was living in Canada, then quickly learned to drive. He approached a friend of his from where he lived in Easton, PA, to embark on what he naively thought would be a quick journey to find the love of his life. Those Greeks are quite the romantics, aren't they? In time, he convinced her to follow him back to the States, where they were married.

Together, my mom and dad were unstoppable. They opened up their first restaurant, then a second, and then a nightclub. With the income from these businesses, finally my dad was able to bring his brothers, sister, and mother to the United States, where he then proceeded to help them achieve their own dreams.

I guess it's in my DNA to follow the same path of my heroes. That entrepreneurial spirit that drove my parents to immigrate to this country, to set up a thriving business, and to find great success in work and in life is the same one that drives me. It's the same one that could drive you, too.

What's so great about business, capitalism, and entrepreneurship—or as I refer to them, "the Holy Trinity of the United States"—is that they work because they are nondiscriminatory. They don't care what gender, religion, or race you are, what language you speak, or even what pursuits you have taken in life. Success and the achievement of your quality of life depends only on *you*. It will help define who and what you are capable of. Everybody has dreams, but what stops people from achieving them? When I was younger, I had a dream of becoming a rock star. In that case, the only thing that stopped me was talent. Or was it because I didn't learn an instrument or want it bad enough?

The dream is the easy part of the journey. All you have to do is close your eyes and put yourself in a happy place. Eventually you do need to wake up. What stops people from pursuing their ambitions? The answer is simple: EFFORT! So the first thing we need to figure out is what it is that makes a person grab that effort.

In my case, when I was young I lost my father—my idol, my hero. I always knew that I wanted to follow in my dad's footsteps. So I stayed in the restaurant business because it felt like the most natural way to communicate with him. Plus, I enjoy people and food and like to bring them together. So I wound up staying in the same career my father had made for himself. But that's not what drove me to the entrepreneurial mindset that we were talking about, or even to starting my own restaurants. More than anything, my entrepreneurial mindset was born out of pain.

I guess I wanted to be like my father a little too soon. I opened my first restaurant when I was only twenty-two. Of course it failed miserably. By the age of twenty-four, I was a failed businessman. I was bankrupt. I'd lost my credit. Lost everything I had. Life could not have been more depressing for me. I was mocked and ridiculed by my family, friends, and people I didn't even know—not only for going into business but for failing. I can assure you, when I think on the pain I suffered back then, it's not the poverty that comes to mind, not even the slightest bit. It was that failure that hurt the most. The failure made me feel cold, naked, and stripped of everything. The worst part was that I didn't know how to tell my mom that I had lost the money she loaned me to set up the restaurant.

Think about that for a moment. My parents came to this country with nothing. They couldn't even speak a word of English. They had no money, no family, and no education, and yet they succeeded. I had more opportunity than they could have ever dreamed about as children, and I lost it all.

The IT Factor

On the day I planned to tell my mother about how I had lost her money, I drove by her apartment and pulled over to the side of the road, not wanting to go in. I didn't know how I was going to break the news to her that not only did I fail, but she was along for my ride in failure.

When I finally worked up the courage to go inside, I said to her, "Mom, it sucks to have to say this, and there is no easy way to say it, but I lost everything for us."

She paused to let it sink in. Then she broke into a smile. "Billy, as long as you have your health and God by your side, you will do well."

In disbelief, I started to say, "But, Mom, I—"

She cut me off with a wave of her hand. "Be an army of one and don't quit. You can fail at what you hate and you can fail at what you love. So why not continue doing what you love? Because as long as you're trying, you're learning to master your craft and getting better at what you love. In the meantime, pain is a part of life. So get used to it!"

That, my friends, is a "Spartan Mom." With her wisdom behind me, I put my head down and went to find a job. Of course I pursued a job as a cook in a restaurant. I'm proud to say that I've never missed a day's work in my life. As long as I can remember, I've always been the first to check in and last to check out. I've never called in sick. At one restaurant in those early years, I got sick while working the line. I'd work sixteen- to eighteen-hour shifts, and toward the end of one of these shifts another cook looked at me and said, "Billy, you look like crap. You're pale. You're sweating. Go outside and get some fresh air." Then he gave me a sandwich he had made in error. Reluctantly I took it and went outside.

When I attempted to eat the sandwich, I'm not kidding when I say that the second I took the first bite, the owner of the restaurant happened to be walking in from his car.

He casually walked up the steps and looked over at me. "You know, Billy," he said, "the reason you have nothing and you lost everything is because you're lazy." Then he took my sandwich and threw it in the trash. "Get back to work or go home," he snapped. "The choice is yours. But I'm not going to pay you to sit and eat."

I had no choice but to go back into work and finish my shift. What could I do? I was scared to lose my job. That was my rock bottom. Everything in my life caused me pain at the time—the loss of my brother, my dad, the loyalty of my friends and family. That day, I felt like driving off a cliff rather than going home. They say that God only gives you what you can handle. I guess God thought I was a badass.

Fortunately, I am blessed to have a strong mom. As they say, the mother's intuition is right, and when I walked through the doors back home, she immediately knew that something was bothering me. I shared the story with her, and the first thing she said was, "You're getting life lessons they don't teach at Harvard. You're getting a master's degree in life." She told me to continue to work hard and focus on being the best at my craft. "No matter how many times you get knocked down, if you look up, you can get up. And I promise you a second opportunity will come your way." She reminded me to be an army of one and not to quit—that quitting is the ultimate failure and that you can either have people look up to you or down on you. "That is your choice," she told me. "But no matter what your decision, you're my son and I love you."

Man, these Spartan women are tough. I had thought that what I needed was a little sympathy, but after speaking with my mom, I swore to myself that I would never again let anyone treat me like my boss had that day. I also promised myself that when I got a second chance at business, I would never treat anyone who worked for me the way I had been treated. *If you ever look down on anyone*, I thought, *then let it be only to lift them up.*

That night, I started thinking about my parents. "What motivated them?" is the question I pondered. Then I found the answer: pain.

Pain is what caused them to leave Sparta, Greece. Pain drove them to pass through Ellis Island and sleep in bus stations and work lowly jobs in other people's restaurants. Dad never wasted an opportunity to learn by looking. While dishwashing, he watched the cooks and learned their art form. Then, as a cook, he watched the managers and learned how to manage. Then he opened his own restaurant and had all the tools he needed to succeed. Then he met my mom and they had this incredible kid named Billy.

I began this chapter by pointing out how grim the job market looks. I did that for one reason: millions of us are suffering these days. Pain is commonplace. I have certainly lived my fair share of it. What matters isn't the pain itself; what matters is what you do with it. I lost a brother, a father, and a business. I dealt with bosses that could not have shown me less kindness. Through it all, yes, I put in the kind of effort it takes to succeed, but more than anything, the pain itself drove me to change my mindset.

My family started in the poorhouse, and we lived our lives as if the poorhouse was following us. Our pain was our driver. Our failure was our humility. Our success was never enough to make us content. As badly as my former bosses treated me, and as much as it hurt to be ridiculed by family and friends, I owe a great deal to them. When I go to church, I light a candle and say thanks for them. If they hadn't been who they were and said what they said, then maybe I wouldn't be doing what I'm doing.

So there you have it. The reason I'm qualified to write on this subject has nothing to do with my education. I am a living, breathing representation of each one of the principles I intend to offer in the pages to come. Those principles led me to the success I'm living today—and they can do the same for you. But before we move on to address them, keep this important opening message in mind: Pain is a part of life. It is what drives us. So get used to it!

Chapter One

The *It* Factor

"An entrepreneur is someone who doesn't have a job."
—Ted Turner

I like that quote, but you know what? I always thought an entrepreneur was something more than that. To me, an entrepreneur doesn't have to be someone who runs a business. He or she can come from any background and be involved in any profession. You know what an entrepreneur is? A person who gets rid of their weakness so they can fight for their dreams or their passions. A person who won't let anyone grind them down. A person who lives a life of passion about what they do for a living. These are the only qualifications for the job. It doesn't matter what you do—if you're passionate and fearless in the pursuit of excellence, then you are an entrepreneur.

When I think about the entrepreneurial mindset, I'm reminded of a couple of things my dad told me when I was growing up. "Billy," he said, "I hope you never find a boss that you like." I didn't understand what that meant until I was older (and by the way, my father's wish came true). What he meant was that he didn't want me to ever feel completely content, because when you're completely content, you stop driving yourself to achieve more than what you already have. When you're content, the entrepreneurial spirit dies. My dad loved business. He saw the good in everyone and opportunities everywhere. He also knew that we lived in a country of endless possibilities, so if I endured some pain in my life, that would drive me to always better myself.

The other thing I remember him saying was, "Some of the most valuable properties in the world are the graveyards because they contain all those buried hopes and dreams of people who didn't make the effort to bring them to life. Those graveyards are filled with musicians, entrepreneurs, artists, and painters who never followed their dreams, so that's where all those dreams go to die." The point here is that, more than anything, you must strive to pursue your dream and make the world a better place.

Now before we move on, let's get one thing straight. We're talking about entrepreneurs and their mindset in this chapter, but that doesn't mean I'm here to tell you how to run your business or how to launch a successful startup or even how to climb the corporate ladder. There are people far more qualified to do that than I am. What I'm here to tell you is that I owe most of my success to one simple concept: I stopped looking at myself as an employee, restaurant owner, or even as an individual and started looking at myself as a business. That's the whole point: if you can shift your mindset to thinking of yourself in a more entrepreneurial way, then you can start having more success and happiness in life and in your career (no matter what it is). I guarantee it.

So with the disclaimer out of the way, what does the mindset look like?

It's More Than a Dream

Author and business coach Brad Sugars once said that "Entrepreneurs are the crazy people who work 100 hours a week so they don't have to work 40 hours for someone else," and he's absolutely right. Entrepreneurs aren't your typical person. We eat, breathe, and sleep our businesses twenty-four hours a day, seven days a week, 365 days a year, and we do so in a way that even the most dedicated employee doesn't. Those of us that run businesses are responsible for our organization's ability to pay bills, pay employees, and pay ourselves while still generating a profit. We are responsible for the health and well-being of the company and its ability to remain relevant and grow. There is virtually no separation between us and our businesses because those two lives parallel one another.

For those that don't own a business, the mindset is basically the same. They are always working, even if that work is simply thinking about how they can improve themselves and further their goals. Their goals are their morning workout. Pursuing them is what they like. For me, I get up and start work immediately because it's what I love. Every morning, I wake up with a goofy smile on my face because I know that today I'll be building my dream and not someone else's. No matter what happens—even if something goes wrong or we face a setback, we don't run from our fears or challenges. We face them. When *I* do that, I know I'll be having a great day, because to me, every day is a payday—that day is about advancing *me by acknowledging and removing my fears.*

Either you pick the career or the career picks you. That's a funny thing about life. Sometimes your career will pick you, and sometimes you pick your career. But in order for that to happen, you need to kill the excuses and keep working. Even if you're not doing what you love right now, the quickest way to figure out what it is you love and need to be doing is by working hard. I was fortunate in that my career was more like a calling . People are always trying to figure things out, but it's that work ethic that decides what direction is best to pursue. It's like this with everything in life: If you want to learn (about yourself, about your career, about how to get better at what you do), then the key is to always keep active.

Always remember that the entrepreneur's mindset is about so much more than just having a dream. If you're going to find success in whatever you do, you need to be patient, have a great work ethic, and have passion about what you do. This means a few things. It means first that you have to be willing to endure some setbacks. Nothing in life or in work is easy (at least not all the time). That's where the patience comes in. Next is that passion. Passion will give you the will to survive those setbacks and help you execute on your dreams. That's a fact. And then there's that work ethic again. Never stop—outwork, outthink, and keep focus until you cross that finish line. Never take a significant break from working on your goals and dreams, and you'll be fine. If you run a business, that means staying involved in all aspects of your business. If you work for someone else, that means remaining passionate about improving yourself and the impact you make on the job and on the people with whom you interact every day.

My passion developed at a young age. When I was growing up, my parents didn't want to let me out of their sight, but at the same time, they had a business to run. That meant I had to sit between the grills and the dishwasher, which wasn't always a pleasant place to be. I'm sure I learned a lot of foul language in both Greek and English. But these drawbacks were nothing compared to the way I felt every time I would enter that diner, surrounded by amazing-looking food and the marvelous smells of my father's ingredients. I loved the way the guests reacted to what my dad created. It was his art, and he was at the top of his game. In this way, food became my passion, and I wanted to sample everything in the restaurant so I could learn how to make it.

The more I studied the art of cooking, the more I realized that every dish in every meal was like a puzzle, and the ingredients were the pieces matched together to form the perfect flavor and visual appeal. There is a certain beauty to the perfect dish, and I became attuned to that beauty in my father's kitchen at a young age.

Today, food for me is a celebration, much like it is for many other people in this country. We eat not merely for survival, but to celebrate life, joy, sorrow, and many other emotions. My father began his life simply hoping to not go to bed hungry, and he fulfilled his dream by helping to satisfy the hunger of others with a true passion for celebrating the culinary arts.

Dreams are nice to have, but they're only a small fraction of the mindset. More important than the dream is the desire to throw yourself into it. This is true no matter what your dream or what you do for a living: The only way you're going to get what you want in life is if you put what you want into it. You've got to combine your passion with your honesty with yourself. I don't just live my work; I *love* it. I'm passionate about it every day. As a result, I get love *out* of my work.

You can either live your dreams or live your fears. The best way to live your dreams is to pursue what you love doing. Love what you do. Be passionate about it. Work hard on it. Life is too short to be miserable. Make these simple changes in your life so you, too, can wake up every morning with a goofy little smile.

It's Not about the Money... But It Also Kind of Is

Since we're on the subject of goals and dreams, ask yourself what it is that you want most. Then ask yourself, "What is that thing worth?" Now, before we get carried away with dreams of riches, let's get one important thing clear: Money is obviously a motivating factor for everyone. We're talking about the pure mindset of an entrepreneur, but we're also not living in a fantasyland here. Money matters. It's just that, here, I'd like to point out that for the most successful people in any profession, success is also measured in dedication to the craft.

People used to say, "The tougher the victory, the sweeter the prize." That's absolutely true. How it applies here is that perfecting your craft is going to take a great deal of hard work and patience. Before you can gain the rewards you seek—whether financial or otherwise—you have to understand and respect this fact. You must understand what you're doing, and more importantly respect it. Combine that with patience and a no-excuses outlook and you will begin earning all those sweet prizes that come with success in your chosen field.

Yes, that success involves money. If you passionately pursue your dream, you will be rewarded financially. That money doesn't often arrive until later in the process, however, so it's important to revel in the other kinds of rewards that show up along the way. Success also means loving what you do. When you love what you do, it becomes a commodity and people want to buy it. Whether it's food, a book, music—when you come to love it is when you start getting paid for it. So your thoughts shouldn't be about the money first, but if you work hard and love what you do, the money comes as a result.

Contrary to what you might have heard about entrepreneurs, money is not usually the central motivating factor. An entrepreneur, no matter what his or her background, cares more about achieving something great—about reaching that dream—than about money. Again, money often comes as part of the reward for that achievement, but it's not what drives this mindset.

If you want a sense of how that moneyless motivation works, consider the stories of the world's greatest companies that started out in garages. Disney, Harley Davidson, Apple, Amazon, Google—these are just a few of the most successful and powerful companies in American history, and they all started in some way or another in a humble working space. They grew into the giants they are today not because they had all the tools and means in the world at the start. Rather, their growth was fueled by a dream, by passion and dedication, and by the pursuit of visionary ideas. Any one of these companies could have folded any number of times when the going got tough, but they all knew that they could and would climb. That's the great thing about starting at the bottom: There's only one way you can go, and that's *up*.

The same was true for hundreds of celebrities who lived paycheck to paycheck (or even in poverty) as they pursued their ultimate dream. Brad Pitt, for example, used to deliver pizzas and wear a chicken suit on the streets for El Pollo Loco. Johnny Depp was a telemarketer who sold pens. Madonna once worked at a Dunkin Donuts before making it big. Michelle Pfeiffer was a supermarket cashier. George Clooney was a tobacco farmhand. You get the idea.

Thinking more generally, recall the stories you've likely heard about rock bands that endured humble beginnings. The Ramones, Nirvana, Creedence Clearwater Revival, The Who, and countless others—the stories are almost always the same. They started off without any money, usually in garages. All they had was their instruments and a passion for making great music. Most bands start out touring in rickety old vans. Most great songwriters begin their songwriting careers performing on street corners. There are stories of rock stars who slept in their cars for years. There are stories about tours that got stranded in the middle of nowhere because the band couldn't make enough money to cover gas to get them to their next gig. At any point, those musicians could have given up and gone to work to collect a paycheck. If money was the motivating factor, that would have been the easiest thing in the world. But they kept on, despite the pain and despite the failure, because they truly loved what they did and wanted to use that love to make a difference in the world.

All these business leaders and actors and musicians—and the tens of thousands of other famous people and successful businesspeople—all embody the spirit of passion for what they do. They are living proof that if it is important to you, then you will find the way. Conversely, the millions upon millions of other people who tried to follow those same paths to success but gave up before they could get there, are testament to what happens when you wind up making excuses and giving up.

This is exactly why money is a motivating factor, but never the central one. People often think that money will free them, but it doesn't. Money is simply a reward for hard, smart work. What truly frees a person is the knowledge that they're doing what they love. They're living and breathing their passion, and that dedication ultimately puts them on the path to success. You hear thousands of stories about famous people who started out with nothing, but only the select few wind up on the screen or playing sold-out stadiums. Those aren't the ones most motivated by money; those are the ones most passionate about achieving their dreams.

Always Be Evolving

In my first business book, *Billy Cooks Like a Mother*, I wrote about a concept called A.B.E. ("Always Be Evolving"). What it means is that the best entrepreneur never stops learning about his role or his industry and evolves as a result. Whenever I think about that need to constantly evolve, I'm reminded of Polaroid. Back in the 80s, their cameras were pretty much everywhere. What wasn't to love? In a world where you had to take a picture on traditional film, fill an entire roll of film, and then wait for that roll to be developed, here you had a device that could show you that picture in a matter of minutes. Plus you got to do that fun dance where you took the photo out and shook it to speed up the development process.

But where is Polaroid now? Sure, they still exist, but they aren't exactly a household name. Most of the time, when people mention Polaroid, the thought that comes to mind is about how great they once were. They failed to evolve with the times, and digital cameras made them obsolete. Now we reminisce more about their contribution to a bygone era than we think about their modern products. That's the lesson: The more you stay the same, the easier it is for your competitors to take you out.

No matter what you do for a living, it's not just about hard work. You can't simply dig ditches and wash dishes. It's about A.B.E., about constantly learning how to get better at what you do and how you can improve your position in your industry. Can you take a class? Can you read a book? Can you discover a new product? Can you become more efficient? Can you apply something in the news to rally your team? These are the kinds of questions that an entrepreneur asks every day. Always Be Evolving.

As the mindset of an entrepreneur evolves, you start to develop your "Spidey-senses." You know the Spiderman bit, right? Part of his superpower is that he can sense when danger is coming. For an entrepreneur, your Spidey-sense means that based on your skillset, you look more to the future and forget more about your past accomplishments. Because you're so focused on the future, you start to see things before they happen. You get that same "Spidey-sense" tingling feeling that something is about to happen, that something needs to be fixed, that you need a new idea to spark positive change. Whatever it is, the senses tingle.

An entrepreneur uses all of his senses. A good entrepreneur has excellent Spidey-sense, and also a great set of eyes. A good entrepreneur needs to be able to look at every aspect of what they do and have an understanding of it. For example, I know how to wait on a table. Sure, my knowledge of it is incomplete—my servers will outrun me every day of the week—but I do know the basics so I can be a person of value to a team member who is sinking.

The Greeks have an expression: "Don't be afraid to work; make work afraid to be near you." That expression doesn't refer to ergophobia (the literal fear of work) either. Obviously we can't be scared to work. No one has ever died from working hard. Stress will kill you. But working hard isn't a killer. As entrepreneurs, we understand innately that we've got to outwork our competitors. We have to be smarter, better, faster. We have to outwork and outperform everyone who does the same thing we're doing.

Rather, what this expression means is that you have to be there to support those around you. And if you want to be there to support those around you, then you can never allow yourself to stop learning.

In many ways, the greatest leaders, managers, and workers of any background haven't mastered any of their trades. They understand all of them, but they have one specialty that is the important part of the engine of their business. But like any great dish, you still have to have a lot of ingredients to be successful, so never be content that you have enough knowledge.

Don't Be Afraid to Knock

Have you ever heard that song "Knock Three Times" by Tony Orlando? Well the lessons from that song about love apply to the mindset, too. I bring it up here because too often I hear from aspiring entrepreneurs that they would love to make progress, but they see no doors opening for them. That's a common misconception, that you have to look for open doors. Here's why it's a misconception: the doors are *never* open. Every door you will ever encounter in your career will be closed. What separates the good entrepreneurs from everyone else is that they aren't afraid to knock. They're even willing to knock three times. The great ones don't only knock, they plow through those doors.

I'm reminded of a story I heard from a Greek friend of mind at the church I attend. The story goes like this: During a war and during a particularly gruesome battle, a soldier was captured and dragged before the enemy's general.

"You have two choices," the general said. "Tomorrow, you can go and be executed by hanging, or you can walk through those doors over there." The general pointed to a pair of heavy iron doors leading out of the fortified compound. The doors were shut tight, but as long as the prisoner knocked, they would open for him.

"What's past those doors?" the soldier asked nervously.

"Nobody knows what's out there," the general said.

The following morning, with the choice between death or facing the potentially terrifying unknown behind those doors, the soldier elected to terminate his life. Willingly he walked to the gallows and let the general hang him.

As the man swung, the general's secretary went to her employer and said, "Why did he choose death? What's behind those doors?"

"Freedom," the general said.

So the prisoner wound up losing his life because of a risk he decided not to take. He was already going to die, but he was more frightened of going through those doors and facing untold horrors, even if his chances of survival may have been better than facing the gallows. That's what happens when people decide not to follow the often intimidating but always more rewarding path that is life and success. They die.

Don't Be Afraid to Fail

What do you want in life? Hopefully that's an easy question for you to answer. Here's a harder one: How badly do you want it? And an even harder one: Are you willing to do what it takes?

As the story of the soldier who chose death teaches us, the most important part of the entrepreneurial mindset is the idea that if you do fail, it's not a big deal, because at least you made the effort. To an entrepreneur, no matter what career he or she pursues, the only real failure in life is to not put in the effort—to wind up swinging from the end of the rope because you were too afraid to try; to wind up in that graveyard full of buried hopes and dreams.

So I'm telling you that you shouldn't be afraid to fail, but don't mistake me: I'm also telling you to do your best to avoid failure. How do you avoid failure? The simplest and best answer is to seek good advice. Here's some more advice, straight from my dad, the ultimate entrepreneur: First, have a great lawyer. Second, have a great CPA. And finally, have a great doctor. His reasoning was that you have to have a support system. I've always followed that rule, and on top of that, I've been fortunate in that I have an ace up my sleeve at all times: My wife and partner Yanna, who I love and adore in everything I do, challenges me daily to be better. That's the best thing an entrepreneur could ever ask for: a challenge.

Nietzsche famously said, "Whatever doesn't kill you makes you stronger." But what he failed to say is, "The stress you do feel *almost* kills you." If you're a motivated individual, disappointment can be completely disorienting. What Nietzsche maybe should have said instead is, "Whatever doesn't kill you makes you watch a lot of old TV reruns and creates a thirst for lots of bad alcohol."

So if you're going to aggressively pursue your dreams, you have to first have an idea of how badly you want them. Next, you have to know what is going to motivate you to succeed. If things don't go exactly right, will you allow those things to create excuses for you to quit? Or will you respect yourself enough to try again and do better next time? It's like my mom said, "It's not about how much respect the world has for you, it's about how much respect you have for yourself." Remember, every day you fight a new battle. You win some, you lose some. That new battle could be with an employee, with a creditor, with your wife, with a friend—you never know. Maybe your best friend tells you your idea is the dumbest thing he's ever heard. Battles come in many different forms. You have to anticipate that they'll happen. Then you also have to know that you don't have to fight every single one of them. Not every battle is important. Some aren't worth fighting. So it's paramount to fight only the battles worth fighting, and then fight them with winning strategies and a strong desire to win.

For me, after I endured that dark period I mentioned in the introduction, from that day forward, if I didn't feel like I had put in a good day's work—if I didn't sweat in the pursuit of my dreams—then I would punish myself by not sleeping. If I didn't work hard enough while I was awake, I figured I didn't deserve to sleep. Obviously that's dangerous and foolish because your brain needs to sleep, but that's what I did when I was a younger man. That drive, focus, and pain is what pushed my wife Yanna and me to open our first restaurant, then our second, and now our third (along with a new concept coming soon to Allentown, PA).

Looking Ahead

With this book, we're going to explore the philosophies above, and many more. Those philosophies can and will help you—no matter what your background or what you do for a living—find greater success in your career and in life. As we move ahead, I'm going to share some stories from my life and about my family.

But this book isn't only about my journey. It's about the journey of every successful entrepreneur who ever lived. I'm no know-it-all. I have embraced philosophies that will work for any entrepreneur. Few people respected me initially, but I followed the lessons from my family, and I found this wonderful woman who loved me, and we built our business on these philosophies. You need to have a good work ethic, ambition, knowledge, and passion. The ambition is the easiest part, but knowledge will give you the confidence to do what you need to do, and passion will ensure that you follow through. This is what allowed us to achieve the American dream, and it's what will allow you to do so, too.

So that's the secret: knowledge. That's it. You have to have the knowledge it takes to succeed as an entrepreneur in whatever field you have chosen for yourself. That's what this book is all about, providing that knowledge. But before we dig into the lessons to come, let me tell you that you won't gain any useful knowledge unless you first have self-respect. When I was failing in business, and even after I found success, I realized that it didn't matter what I did. I knew that, even if I gave 100%, there was always going to be someone I worked for or with who still wouldn't appreciate my effort. Your bosses, your coworkers, the people following your career—they're never going to see that you have given your full effort because seeing that is not their top priority. They have their own responsibilities. And this forces them to count on you for other responsibilities. This is why self-respect is so important: If you don't have the self-respect it takes to succeed, those opinions will drag you down long before you can achieve your dreams.

For these reasons, our next two chapters discuss trust and dealing with the negativity of other people in your lives. These two concepts help you build the kind of self-respect you need to succeed—the kind of self-respect that makes you invincible, the kind of person who can't be knocked down because other people don't like you or approve of how you do your job. Not everyone likes my food, but I know I do my best, and that's why I'm still relevant in this industry. Self-respect has to come first. Much has changed since my parents first came to this country and opened their own business. Hell, much has changed since I opened *my* first business. But that central lesson remains the same: With the right mindset—one that thinks entrepreneurially and has plenty of self-respect—*anyone* can find great success in work and in life.

Chapter Two
If You Can't Be Trusted on the Small Things…

"Remove your weaknesses so you can focus on your fight."
—Billy Kounoupis

That's right. I'm going to start out the chapter by quoting myself. It's my book, so I might as well quote from my previous work. The point in the above quote is clear: As you continue on your journey, you now understand that you should never waste your pain. Rather, the goal should always be to make something great come out of it. Think about a mother's pain as she gives birth. That's a physical pain beyond anything a non-mother like me can imagine. But out of that pain comes a baby, the most beautiful blessing of all. A mother endures all this discomfort for nine months, then the searing pain of labor. She's pushing, she's tired, she's overwhelmed by all that pain, and when it's over, she has a baby. It's a life-changing moment where she sees the world in a new light.

That day I was sick and had a boss tell me I was lazy was a painful moment that shaped who I am and what I do today. And that certainly wasn't the only painful moment I had to endure as a person and as a business leader. My journey has made me realize and never forget that my failures were not the opposite of my success, but a part of my success.

In this chapter and the chapters to come, we're going to continue turning that focus inward. Now we have come to the time when you must learn to understand yourself and what you need to do. How does that work? It begins by understanding that you are not just an individual, you are a *leader*. Whether you lead a group of employees or not is irrelevant. You could be a nurse or a schoolteacher, a lawyer or a dentist, a startup entrepreneur or a restauranteur. You can even be unemployed at the moment. The best way to learn about yourself is to *lead* yourself to that discovery. And the best way to reach the next level in whatever you do is to *lead* yourself to that next level.

How do we do that? Well, it all starts with an acronym: FACE. That stands for "Focus, Attitude, Commitment, and Ethics." That's just one of the many Billy-isms I'll throw at you with this book, but I like to think of this one as foundational. Always remember to save FACE, and you'll be well on your way to success.

Focus

Two components are key to maintaining your focus as a leader and as a person. The first is to create and maintain a plan. The second is to manage your time appropriately. You've heard these concepts before, and yet it is so difficult for many people to follow through on them.

For me, I started with a basic outline about what I needed in order to achieve my goals. In my case—and in my opinion, this should be the same for everyone, no matter who they are or what they do—the most important part of the outline was to always make sure I set aside time to work on my health. I built in time to stretch, walk, maintain good hygiene (which is sometimes tough when you're working eighty-hour weeks), and so on. The second part of my outline involved opportunities to seek knowledge. I always make sure to read the newspapers every morning. How else am I supposed to know what's going on in my community, my industry, or with the people in and around my businesses? Those were my two core values: health and knowledge. In other words, my entire philosophy was and always has been based around walking and reading.

Why is this so important? Well, getting outside and knowing about what's going on around you can lead to opportunities you would never encounter sitting at a desk and focusing on your daily tasks. For example, one morning I read in the newspaper that a restaurant in Allentown had closed up because they lost their liquor license. Since I had a deep knowledge of my industry, I realized that there are only two reasons you can lose such a license: either you get caught admitting minors or you fail to pay your taxes. With a little more research into the matter, I discovered that this particular restaurant had faced the tax issue. Because I read the paper that morning, I found a formerly successful restaurant that wouldn't be able to continue in business because of one big mistake.

So I went up to find the location. I looked around the property and drove through the community. By the time I was done, I was completely in love with the place. I set up a meeting with the landlord for the next day. Long story short, because of the knowledge I gained from taking the time to read the paper, I wound up making a deal on one of the most profitable restaurants I own today.

I'm not going to tell you exactly what to write into the outline that will help bring you your focus, but I will tell you that exercise and reading will transform you almost immediately. It's the quickest path to change, and it also happens to cost you almost nothing at all. You have to make a commitment to these two elements—and for some people, that commitment is difficult—but they can be life changing and career changing. Beyond these components, creating your outline is a matter of knowing your passion and building what you're passionate about into the outline.

The next important factor is time. Don't waste time. You can buy anything, but you can't make up for lost time. If I feel like spending the money, I can buy the world's shiniest and fastest car, but no matter how much money I make, I can't buy a twenty-fifth hour in the day. Once that hour, that day, or that week is gone, it's gone, and that is an incredibly valuable thing to waste. So when you look at your outline, be sure to prioritize your day—and I'm not talking about laundry or washing your car; I'm talking about treating yourself like an executive with a purpose. Prioritize all those things that will take you to the next level as a person and a leader in your career.

Attitude

I love the word "attitude." This word is so *essential* to life. Good attitude, bad attitude—this is a word that has a unique meaning to everyone. To me, attitude is more like a combination of words. It combines the knowledge of what is right, what is humble, what is loving, and what shows respect. If you do what is right, humble, loving, and respectful, then your attitude is good. If not, then it's time for a course correction.

When you focus on your goals and achieve success as a result, the people around you might appear to change. They will start to view you differently and treat you differently. In your mind, you won't see anything wrong with how you're behaving—after all, you've always lived life with that right attitude. But these outsiders will see your success as going to your head. They will say that you only care about work and have forgotten your friends. They will say things like, "I never see you at the club anymore. What happened to you?" The best thing to do here is to bite your tongue instead of saying something like, "Well, I never see you at the bank either. So what happened to *you?*" Believe me, I've thought about saying that kind of thing dozens of times. But part of the attitude is to be humble, so words like these don't fit. You don't want to look like a snob but like someone who values her time. Don't flaunt your success. Simply keep your head high and be happy that you're doing a job you love and making progress.

Commitment

Speaking of progress, let's talk about commitment. We all make New Year's resolutions, but how many of us keep them? I used to make a resolution every year to quit smoking. For years, I would never succeed. Eventually I turned to self-deprecating humor to mask my disappointment. I would say to my friends, "Quitting smoking is easy. I've done it hundreds of times before." When it came to my weight, my wife Yanna would say to me, "Billy, get in shape." And I would say, "Round is a shape." I did everything I could to mask my failures with humor. My pain was my friends' entertainment. Meanwhile, behind closed doors, I was disgusted with myself. I hated looking in the mirror because I could see how completely I was lying to myself.

Eventually I knew I had to change at any cost. So I made myself a promise that I would never say "tomorrow" and push it off to the side. I changed my common phrase of procrastination to expressions like, "There is no tomorrow," "We live in the now," and "Now I will change." Eventually I realized that I hadn't achieved the changes I wanted because I lacked commitment.

How could I embark on my journey as a professional or an entrepreneur (or anything really) if I couldn't commit to stop what was destroying me from the inside out? I had to do more than just try to build my business from a leadership position; I had to lead myself toward better choices in life. I had to commit to being a better person, to living healthier, and to counting on myself for the small things before I could ever start counting on myself for the big things. That first step was to commit. I had to make a commitment to myself and to my future. Once I did that, quitting smoking finally stuck—and all at once, I started meeting my personal and professional goals.

Ethics

You know what always amazes me about the subject of entrepreneurship? Most people don't know (or sometimes they forget) what an entrepreneur really is. As an entrepreneur, you realize what you do and how you run your business is a reflection of you. You have to remember that what you do is going to have a great effect in your community. It's not only about creating a great business; it's about making a positive impact on the people around you.

For example, my restaurants are a destination. My community brings people to me and I bring people to my community because of my work ethic and my family's work ethic, because of our love and passion for what we do, and because we care a great deal about our community. As entrepreneurs, we understand that we're boosters for our communities. This is the case with most places: they all revolve around the contributions of their entrepreneurs. Think of the famous restaurant rows in Chicago, Philadelphia, New York, and so on. Think of every retail district in any city you've ever been to. They all have jewelry districts, garment districts, market districts, etc. These districts and the communities within them all owe much of their identity to the entrepreneurs that brought people together into a community and a common cause.

A true entrepreneur considers himself an artist. A creator. An innovator. A leader. But he is also responsible for not only himself, but his community, as well. This often means that an entrepreneur is a leader who must put work and those for whom they are responsible before themselves. I've been in business for thirty years, and in that time, I've never done anything other than work in or own restaurants. One thing I can tell you with the utmost honesty: I care more about my employees than they do about me. And I know this because I make more commitments to them than I do to myself.

What do I mean here? I mean that there's a tradeoff between not only doing the right thing, but also remembering that, long before I worry about paying the mortgage or paying myself, I have to make sure my staff gets paid. I make sure they're always taken care of. This doesn't make me special, by the way. It just makes me an entrepreneur. Money isn't the central motivating factor; using my dream to improve the world is the central motivating factor. A big part of that is always making sure that I take care of the people I count on. It's also important to keep in mind that the stress that comes with that is non-negotiable. It just comes with the territory.

When we talk about taking care of the community you count on, you have to have an understanding of yourself before you can put others first. Think about it like this: What a leader does is connect the dots. She makes connections between people and services, problems and solutions, and makes everything work in a more harmonious way. She almost creates, for lack of a better word, *marriages*. There are marriages between the boss and employee, the teacher and pupil, trainer and trainee, and so on. A leader also creates healthy marriages between the representatives of their business and the customers. Like a marriage, these relationships have their ups and downs, their good times and tough times. Leading a group of people that counts on you isn't always sunshine and roses.

The Greeks have an expression: "A good captain shows his skills during stormy weather." If you don't know how to deal with that stormy weather, and if you haven't trained your mindset on how to get through the tough times, then you will find it difficult to put someone else first. So before you can get to that point as a great leader where you're putting other people first, you must have a great understanding of what you're doing. You can't lead effectively if you don't know where you're going, after all.

And like the ocean brings tides, you'll experience lots of high tides and low tides. Expenses come in like tides. Problems, too. Whether the electricity goes out at your store, employees hurt themselves, someone tries to steal something, someone doesn't show up for their shift, or so on—high tides and low tides will come and go. Sometimes you feel like those high tides are rarer than the low ones. This is when you will understand the difference between doing what is right and doing what feels good. To do what is right is to stand out front with your ship and crew, communicate your needs properly, and be responsible for making sure everyone has what they need to succeed.

You've heard the saying that life imitates art? Well, the same applies in business. Business imitates life; life imitates business. The fact is, whether you run your own business or not, you are responsible to your community. It's all part of being human. If you're an entrepreneur running a business, you're responsible for your organization's ability to pay bills, pay employees, pay yourself, and still generate a profit.

If you're an entrepreneur working for someone or with someone else, you have a responsibility to take care of the others in your life before you take care of yourself.

Along the way, you've got to realize that sometimes you have to make sacrifices, and more importantly, that those sacrifices won't kill you. When my wife Yanna and I were building the restaurant called Billy's, we turned off our phone at home, we sold the TV, we got rid of cable, we went down to one cell phone, we strictly budgeted our groceries, and on and on. Those sacrifices didn't kill us. If you're smart, when you're talking about sacrifice, you realize that your journey is going to be tough and you'll have to make sacrifices, but they're not going to put an end to you. Think about it this way: Did my father's sacrifice of leaving his home country to go to a place where he had no money and didn't speak the language kill him? Or did it make him better?

I've known restaurant owners who would sleep in the basement of their restaurants, snuggled up with the potatoes and onions. They might have faced hardships, but they weren't going to make an excuse. They would be there, steering the ship. They were responsible for the health and well-being of the enterprise, and for the company's ability to remain relevant and grow.

I live and breathe my business not only because I want to do better, but because these are the obligations and promises I make to the people I depend on and work with. It's the same in any industry and any setting. The entrepreneurial spirit is one that values the people on whom you depend.

It is important to remember that, although education is paramount, the ethics you follow will always supersede that. You can have the best and broadest education in the world, but if you're not a good person who follows the highest ethical standard, it doesn't matter. Think about every high-level scandal of the past decade. Usually a smart person or persons did the wrong thing and got caught. Think about Michael Milken. John DeLorean. Bernie Madoff. Smart guys, all of them. And although they were highly educated, failing to do the right thing brought them crashing down. They lost everything—their fortunes, their companies, their families, their reputations, their *freedom*—and they lost it completely. They all chased wealth at the expense of the principles of FACE, and look what happened.

So always remember that wealth isn't only money. What is the value of money to Bernie Madoff now? Wealth is family, friends, education, and peace of mind. As always, the value is inside you. Always save FACE. It's the best way to protect yourself, your family, your brand, and everything you do, and it's the best way to ensure success in *all* manners of wealth.

Chapter Three
Dealing with Poison

"Show me your friends and I will show you who you are."
—God

Here I am having fun again with the opening quote. I've never met God personally, so I can't tell you for sure whether I'm attributing that quote correctly. What I can tell you is that the above is a paraphrase of Proverbs 13, verse 20. "Whoever walks with the wise becomes wise, but the companion of fools will suffer harm." The message is clear: The people you associate with tend to define you. Hang out with good people, and you'll be a good person. Hang out with bad people, and you'll probably not be the greatest company. Spend your time with dreamers who never do anything about their dreams, and you'll be stuck in a rut forever. But if you spend time with positive people who believe in what you're doing . . .

That's what we're going to be discussing in this chapter: How to deal with the various poisons in our lives—whether they are distractions, bad habits, or people, they're going to bring you down. And when you achieve your success, that's the last thing you want.

Here's something you may not know about success: It never goes unnoticed. Greatness is never ignored. When you find success, that's when the floodgates open. People will begin congratulating you.

They'll tell you they always believed in you (even if you know that isn't the case). Then, inevitably, people will start to ask for money or partnership in business ventures. The funny thing about when this happens is that you hear yourself being congratulated all the time and you don't know why because you're too busy living your life to even know that you're successful.

Whenever I think about that little nugget of wisdom, I'm reminded of a story Tony Orlando told me. He said he once went to visit James Taylor in the rundown apartment where he lived at the time. This was long before his commercial success, of course. Tony said to James, "Play me what you think is your very best song." James played something that Tony said he doesn't even remember now. It wasn't good enough to register. Then Tony said, "Play me your least favorite song." That's when James played "Fire and Rain," which if you're not a fan of his music, let me tell you, that became a huge hit. *Rolling Stone* ranked it among the top 500 songs of all time. James Taylor had a successful song and he didn't even *know it* yet.

But that is not the focus in this chapter. The focus is on the poison that can come into your life when you start making the kinds of strides we're striving to make. Once you take that next step between finding something that will make you successful and achieving that success, that's when you learn who your true friends are. They aren't the ones asking for loans or jobs or any other kind of financial leg-up. True friends don't ask anything of you. The ones that do? Those are the poisonous ones, and I'm here to tell you that a huge part of managing success—really, it's a much, much bigger part of it than I wish it was—is about how you deal with the poison.

God and the Magician

There was a time in my life when I lost faith in God, family, and everything around me. When my priest learned the state I was in, he offered to tell me a story. It was a story about the importance of faith in business and in life.

Here's how the story went: There once was a magician who achieved a deep mastery of both illusion and science. In his mind, there was nothing that he could not make happen, whether by physical means or mystical. That magician was so confident that he went up to God and said, "God, anything you can do, I can do too. What you do is no big deal."

God looked down at the magician and smiled. "That's interesting," He said. "Should we put that claim to the test?"

The magician puffed out his chest. "Absolutely," he said. "I'm ready. Give me your best shot."

So God stooped down and picked up a handful of dirt. He rubbed it around in his palms for a moment before blowing into it, and—boom!—where once was a cloud of dust now stood a man. "There," God said. "I have created a man."

The magician scoffed. "Is that all you have for me?" He shook his head incredulously. "I can do that same thing with science." He then knelt and began gathering some dirt at God's feet, just as God had done.

God held out a hand to stop the magician. "Wait," He said. "If you believe that you can do anything I can do, then you must first make your own dirt."

Realizing he was beaten, the magician stepped back and gave reverence to God.

In this story, a magician tries to imitate God, but quickly learns that this is impossible, because God created everything. Similarly, in faith, in business, and in life, only one person can deliver the goods truly and properly. That person is you. When you have faith in what you're doing and you believe it, you know that you can't have someone pull the wool over your eyes. This is when you know you are approaching your graduation to the level of a true entrepreneur.

In the creation of your journey, and as your story is written, your value and your strength is in your understanding of self. "Give me a hundred thousand dollars," someone says, "so we can start a business and change the world." When that person approaches you, looking for a handout, you're going to look at them differently, just as God looked at that magician. This is because *you* have created your business, transformed yourself, and learned that there is no easy way to do anything. There's just a lot of redundancy and patience. These people who approach you in this way? They need to learn that they have to make their own dirt.

Keep Your Head Down

In my time as a businessman, I've met many immigrants who own businesses, and I've always been amazed at how often a foreign-born entrepreneur seems to find success. Think about it. Here you have someone who was born in another country, so this person begins her life as an entrepreneur at a disadvantage. She doesn't know everything there is to know about the culture; she often doesn't have the same kind of education we get here in the US; and she is almost always up against a language barrier. So how is it that, despite those obstacles, so many of them succeed in building great businesses (and businesses that often last for generations)?

The answer is simple: more often than not, an immigrant entrepreneur understands the value of hard work. He had to work hard just to get to this country, and then had to work hard to make ends meet, and then had to work hard to raise enough money and time to get a business started. Once the business is up and running, the hard work doesn't stop. Equally important, the entrepreneur values what they have built to the point where they protect it at all costs. You can't put one over on someone like this. They're skeptical about "opportunities" brought forward by poisonous people. They work hard every day. The glass is never half full or half empty; it's half water and half air. They're able to grow because of their patience and understanding and their different views of the world.

So the lesson we can learn from the immigrant entrepreneur is to work hard, even when you have found success. People will approach you when you become successful, and the best way to keep them out of your way is to keep your head down and work. When I was struggling in business, nobody wanted anything to do with me. Then, when we started winning awards and gaining recognition, the same people who ignored me or looked down on me came back and told me how they always knew I would be successful and how they couldn't wait to do business with me now. I have stepped around them every time, and the way I've done that has been by keeping my head down and sticking to working on what I know.

Negativity

Negative people get that way in part because they believe that the world is "supposed to be" one way or another, and their views of the way the world actually is don't align with that "supposed to be." Some think that the way the world is supposed to work is that you go to school, get a good education, land a job working for someone else, strive to make and save tons of money, and so on. But where is it written that this is the only reasonable path? Screw that. Don't let the "supposed to" dictate your life.

Quality of life doesn't come from dollars. Don't get me wrong; you can have a good time being miserable with lots of money, but people forget that material things like houses and cars are only a temporary fix. You can make all the money in the world and buy as many houses as you want, but the most valuable commodity (other than time) is happiness. Don't be the person who knows the price of everything and the value of nothing. Don't be the person who wastes your time and even your life on something you hate. And pay no attention to the negative people around you who tell you that you can't do what you want to do or will fail if you try.

You must live and breathe this as if your life depends on it, because it does. My life as a restauranteur depended on it. I never would have made it in this line of work if not for that piece of wisdom. I learned that the negative can only weigh you down, that it's more important to understand and know what you have as opposed to the "supposed to be" or "what if." For example, I worry about the customers I have, not the ones I don't. What does that mean? It means I make sure my foundation is solid. If you do that in your own life, whatever you do, trust me, your base will bring in new customers or new opportunities.

As an aside, I wish I could say that every idea is mine in our business, but the fact is we've learned a lot from our customers. It's not just on the basis of what we did, but on the knowledge we gain from them. This is one of the reasons we learned early on that we needed to always love and respect our guests.

Through it all, keep in mind that there will be people who will try to take your mind off the path. These people are almost always negative and their words poisonous. They'll always tell you why something won't work or encourage you to take the easy way. If you feel them starting to get to you, the way to stride back to the path is to not lose faith—both in yourself and in your higher power.

Your Journey Comes Alive

The final lesson in our chapter on dealing with poison is that you have to have faith. Now I'm not going to tell you what religion you need to be or what your picture of God should be, only that it's important to believe in something bigger than yourself, and to trust that that something will always provide if you work hard enough.

When I was growing up, my father was a huge Tony Orlando fan. In my house, we watched *Happy Days*, we appreciated Sonny and Cher, and my dad absolutely loved Tony Orlando (partly because he was half Greek). Those were the good old days. To Dad, Tony Orlando was bigger even than Elvis.

Award Winner Tony Orlando and JD Sarantakos presenting Billy with award

Fast forward to the present. As fate would have it, a cousin of mine, JD, found himself working as the manager for Tony Orlando himself. My cousin called me up not long ago to say that Tony's camp had decided to take his Christmas show to Bethlehem, PA, given how reminiscent of Christmas the town's name happened to be. Since I am so connected in the region around Bethlehem, my cousin hoped to get some insight from me on where they might stage the show. So I called one of my friends, Jeff, who is part owner of a popular event center in Bethlehem where some of the largest acts in the world have performed—everyone from Rod Stewart to Janet Jackson to Motley Crue to Hollywood Vampires, to mention a few. In this way, we connected the dots and managed to bring my father's idol in to do his show.

Wouldn't you know it? We wound up doing a welcome party for Tony in one of my restaurants. And wouldn't you know it? Tony even asked my daughter Georgia if she would be willing to sing with the choir he would have on the show, and my son Michael if he would be willing to play the role of the little drummer boy and the dreaded elf. That was how, with one fateful phone call, I went from respecting my dad's appreciation of Tony Orlando to watching my children perform on stage with him.

So was this coincidence or a matter of fate? I might be more inclined to believe the former if I was living in Los Angeles or traveling in the same circles as Tony Orlando. But here, it all started because of this little hole-in-the-wall of a restaurant I purchased sixteen years ago. I strongly believe that it is my faith as an entrepreneur, coupled with my faith in God, that has led me to everything I have wanted. I have always felt that God is listening to me. He has answered all of my questions (it's just that a lot of the time, He happens to say no).

For example, when I was younger, I dreamed of being a teacher. Of course I never became a teacher, but the funny thing is that I'm asked to speak in schools and colleges all the time. I went to college and failed in writing and math, and now I'm working on my third book, and on top of that, my business life revolves around math. I wanted to marry a person who would be like me, and still better, and I got exactly that.

So all those things I wanted when I was a kid, I wound up getting. Now that I'm in my fifties, all my prayers from when I was young are being answered. But it wasn't until they started coming to fruition that I remembered my requests. Whatever your faith is, it seems pretty clear in my case that my desires were *heard*. But what the hell do I know? I'm fifty-one and I still flip eggs.

Chapter Four
Understanding Your World

"Show me disloyalty and I will show you detachment."
—*Some Smart Person*

The next phase of the journey we're on here is to understand your place in the world. The first step is to recognize that the world is a better place because you live in it. For example, in my diner, the experience isn't only about the food; it's about the people, and realizing that sometimes you need to go beyond food. It sounds funny, but in life and business, you need a foundation, and you need to know the positivity you bring to the table, and in how many ways you can bring it there.

Think about a customer in a diner. That person might arrive looking down in the dumps. Or maybe that person is upset, but not outwardly so, and treats her server with negativity. The typical human reaction is to respond in kind. But at my diner, I tell my staff that we always have to remember that we're dealing with a person here, not just a customer. Who knows why this person is feeling or reacting this way? She might've had a fight with her spouse, might be going through a divorce, might have just suffered a death in the family, and so on. With that in mind, I have always felt that it is my obligation and my team's obligation to touch everyone that comes through our door and show them a good experience, no matter what.

The title of this chapter is "Understanding Your World." Think about that for a minute. "*Your* World." No, it's not a fantasy. It is not the world that creates us; it is we who create our own world. Think about it this way: We're not talking about being a ruler of time and space; we're talking about *creating* space for ourselves.

Allow me to explain. We create our own world through the choices we make. You can choose where you want to live, how you want to live, who you want to associate with, and on and on. Now keep in mind that you have to make all these things happen. I simply can't say this enough: Life doesn't give you what you want; it gives you what you deserve. Once you can grasp that fact, that's when you now know that you are capable of making the world a better place.

Let's look at it on a smaller scale. Think about a teacher in a public school. Are they the highest paid people in the world? Unfortunately no. But can you deny the lives they touch? Of course not. Many teachers change the way their students think about school and the joy of learning. Some of them serve as a bright light in an otherwise dark upbringing. Some inspire their students to become great people, to become doctors, even presidents.

The Impact of Simple Gestures

Now, I don't want to seem like I'm writing a book to promote my restaurants (I'm really not, I swear); it's just that my own career serves so often as a nice metaphor for the advice I have to give. So please bear with me through another restaurant analogy. In my world of restaurants, giving good food is paramount. But let's assume I have the best food imaginable, but my staff ignores the customer—or worse, disrespects them. How important is my food now? And how important is the price of the meal?

This is exactly why I promote the same "understand your world" principles with my staff as I'm sharing with you today. Let me explain: The minimum wage the state requires me to pay my servers is $2.83 an hour. At that rate, do you think they're working for me because I'm Brad Pitt's twin brother? Heck no! And do you think they only make $2.83? Of course not. They make their tips from the service they provide. The better they know the product, the warmer their smile, the more engaging they are with the customer, the more money they make.

Now that's what they bring to the table. Here is what I bring: leadership, organization, marketing, and a hard work ethic. That brings us to another point—the combination of my working on my craft for over thirty years, combined with my staff's willingness to work and be professional, allows them to make even more money than kindness alone could deliver. My staff is better educated than most. I have servers with MBAs and psychology degrees; I employ teachers, artists, and musicians. Serving tables is what they do in my restaurant, but it's not who they are. The truly successful ones know they are entrepreneurs—they are a business unto themselves. How does the environment my restaurants provide them make their world better? They learn the skills it takes to succeed in anything. They have opportunities to bring money home. And in return, they work hard and well, and they have touched my life as well.

Solid Roots

What's important in my world? The simple gestures. The people, work ethic, being smart, family, loyalty, music, art, food, and respect—I have created my world, and I choose who I want in it. When it comes to my customers, I choose to make a difference. My world has most definitely touched their lives, as they have inspired mine. The fact is that I can't wait to see them every day, and I know the feeling is mutual. They could go anywhere to eat, but they come to me and wait in lines for a joke, coffee, food, or simply a smile. And I wake up early to go and see them seven days a week.

It's funny; my world started with me, my wife Yanna, one cook, two servers, and one dishwasher, and now we are approaching 130 employees, and my locations serve thousands of people per week. And how did it all start? From the hundreds of people that touched my life— from my teachers at Easton High School to my cousins with whom I have spent time talking about the dream, to the people that mentored me as to how to build the dream. As I said earlier, there were times I wanted to drive off a cliff, but thankfully, I was blessed to have a few heroes in my life, and I would like to think that I have helped change other people's lives. I would like to think that my crew has, too. And you, the reader, as well. It doesn't matter if you didn't cure cancer. It doesn't matter if you don't have millions of dollars. Heck, it doesn't even matter if you graduated from high school. None of that means that you haven't done your share. It just means that you are so caught up in other things that you forget how great you really are.

How Do You Want to Be Portrayed?

Near the time of this writing, one of the greatest rock musicians of all time passed away. Prince was legendary in so many ways. His music inspired and challenged and entertained millions, and his guitar playing was out of this world. Nearly everything he did was flamboyant, yes, but it was also carefully calculated and maintained with purpose. A large part of that calculation he dedicated to his image. Many people think he changed his name to an unpronounceable symbol so he could regain the rights to his given name and persona, but what I'm talking about is much smaller than that.

Prince traveled with an entourage, as many entertainers tend to do. But what Prince did differently is that he always required his followers to dress well. They weren't allowed to wear jeans. He didn't want to project the image that he surrounded himself with people smoking cigarettes, wearing ripped T-shirts, and displaying piercings and tattoos. He saw his entourage as a part of his own image. They were, to him, quite literally a representation of the world he created for himself. The lesson from Prince is that whether you're a superstar, a frontline employee, or a mechanic is irrelevant. How do you want to be portrayed? That's what matters.

In my restaurant, I require all my employees to use cordial language at all times. I have the highest standards for how they must dress and act, right down to the smallest chip in a server's nail polish. The house has to be perfectly clean and sanitary.

On the business side, I have ways to build this perfect world we always strive for. Good food. Good music. Exceptional, smooth service. We train our people to give sincere compliments and always look for the good in every customer. I tell them that what might be minutiae to you could mean a lot to them. You don't know how much time this woman spent on looking good, for example. Her husband might not even have noticed, but now this stranger notices. Of course this impacts them in a positive way. That just made this person's world a little better.

The message has resonated so much that many of my servers take the lessons into their everyday lives. I have one server who has been with my restaurants for eleven years. The money she has made on the job has obviously helped her, but the new mindset she has developed has taken it all much farther than money ever could. She now views herself as a business. She lives in a great home in the same community I live in. She's highly educated with a master's degree. And it is all because she started looking at herself differently when she learned that, with a little effort, you can make your own world whatever you want it to be.

The fact is that life is not a dress rehearsal. If you don't know what type of world you want, then simply do the right thing, trust the process, and let God write your story. Your life, your world, your choice. Whichever way you go, don't make excuses.

I don't want to keep beating a dead horse until it's glue, so I'll leave you with this one last piece of wisdom. You do make the world a better place because you live in it.

Chapter Five
Originality

"If you want to be original, be ready to be copied."
—*Coco Chanel*

Damn, I wish that was my quote. What an excellent summary of the point we're about to explore here. Think about how powerful that statement is. Originality is something to aspire to, but it's also something that makes you somewhat of a target. If you blaze trails, many people are going to follow you. Sometimes they'll try to take what you've done and create a strange and cheap imitation of it. The first trick is not to let it bother you. The second is to keep yourself and your ideas fresh. This way, even when someone else renders your work less original, you keep moving ahead to new originality.

With a name like Basilis Panayiotis Kounoupis, I knew from a young age that I was going to be original. And I also knew that I was going to probably get beaten up in school. At one time I was five feet tall and 140 pounds, and I had that unusual name. Unless you're Greek, that name was exactly that same kind of target I mentioned in the first paragraph. Trust me, at age ten, I didn't want to be original. That desire got even stronger by the time I reached high school. The thing is, though, if you're not an original—if you don't embrace your remarkable (and *useful*) weirdness on the outside—then what you become is a follower. Following is easy. There is no effort. Being original and embracing your originality is the ultimate compliment you can give to yourself because it means you are honest with yourself. This is a great gift, as it will most assuredly make you a happier person.

Even back when I was getting picked on in school, I could sense that originality was always a positive trait. I also learned that it's okay if you feel like you need a moment to sulk and feel sorry for yourself once in a while. I say go for it. After all, that's the only way you can grow up. We're not in high school anymore, of course, but there's always plenty of growing to do. It's important to remember that challenges aren't there to stop you; they're there to help you grow.

The Genuine Article

Creativity and originality—these are the key components in life, relationships, and business. They are part of your spirit, your *soul*. The bad news is that they can't be bought. The good news, though, is that everyone has them. It's just a matter of growing them, fostering them, and making them work for you.

Let me clarify. These words about creativity and originality mean nothing without action and implementation. Action you know. But *implementation*—that's what gives these words their greatest value. An entrepreneur tends to be extremely creative and original in spirit. He can create products and services you didn't even know you needed, and can create brands you trust. But not every entrepreneur succeeds.

The ones that do succeed have that originality and creativity in spades, but they also owe much of their success to action and implementation. Look at Steve Jobs, Ralph Lauren, Henry Ford. These men were (and are) the epitome of originality. Their brands succeeded because they were true to their vision and were determined to implement it.

The link between truth and originality is important and sincere. It creates a genuine bond of emotion, intellect, and trust that rings true in our lives. There is no substitute, no matter how the copycats and fakers may try to exploit that trust, steal ideas, and create forgeries. Picture that knock-off Rolex or those not-quite-the-genuine-article designer clothes. You can wear them. You can even appreciate them. But they're not the original, and they'll never connect with you on that same emotional level that the true or the genuine would.

Here's another fact I learned: no one likes a phony. It doesn't matter who you are or what your position in life—if you're a phony, that's far worse than anything someone could mock or ridicule you for. Anyone who has ever built anything, created something great, and/or knows who they really are share one important thing in common: they don't suffer these kinds of fools. Yeah, anyone you could ever want to associate with, do business with, or work for or with would agree. No one wants the phony.

Imagine you walk into an art museum, and you encounter room after room full of stunning masterpieces painted by some of history's greatest artists. Then, you stumble into the gift shop, where you see all these Picasso paintings for sale in poster form. The reprinted, phony representation is never even close to as awe inspiring.

These are truths we all recognize and have come to know. But too few instantly recognize that the inverse of this is also true. If you encounter someone who is a little off-centered—someone who doesn't conform to every last normalcy of the world and the culture we have constructed—but that person is obviously being true to themselves, then you tend to respect them. You respect them even if you don't immediately realize it. This is because, far more than conformity and far more than pretending to be what you think people want you to be, genuineness is appreciated. Weird originality trumps phony conformity every time. Respect always follows the genuine article.

The deeper message here is that being comfortable with who you are allows you to grow. Copying someone else, meanwhile, will only set you back and eventually render you obsolete. Most people can spot a phony, and most people distance themselves from phonies.

The lesson, then, is to focus on being you. Don't simply go through the motions. Have a true understanding of yourself. If you're truthful and you focus on your originality, people will trust you and your journey toward the life you choose. And you know what? The truer you are to yourself, the easier everything will be along the way.

Focus on Being Yourself

Being comfortable with who you are allows you to grow. Copying someone else will set you back; it will make you obsolete. Think about it this way: If you want to catch some live music tonight, would you rather go see a tribute band or the band who created the music that tribute band is covering? Of course you would prefer to see the original.

So why then do so many people focus on trying to be something they're not—or worse, trying to be someone else entirely? It's like everyone everywhere is trying to be a cover band. There's good reason for this, I suppose. Being a cover band is safer. There's less risk of bombing out and failing if you know for certain that the songs you're playing will resonate with the audience. But your ceiling as a cover band is extremely limited. You'll never taste even a fraction of the success of the original.

Let's agree to stop playing cover tunes. While the rest of the world is jamming to someone else's originality, focus on being yourself. It's like my grandmother used to say: The fingers on your hand aren't all the same size, so why would people be? Everyone is unique and different. So while everyone else is trying to conform and be the same size as those who succeeded, you be different. Understand that you're unique. Be yourself. Do this, and *you* become the genuine article. You may stumble a few times along the way, but don't worry—all the greats stumbled. Keep focusing on your originality and making it the best it can be, and you too will succeed in whatever it is you choose to do.

Chapter Six
Make Your Own Path

"There is always something worth fighting for."
—*Billy*

If you're making your own path, as I have chosen to do in life—and as I encourage everyone to do—then you need to act when the opportunity arises. If you find the right job, you take it. If you find the right girl, you marry her. If you find the right house, you put in an offer. Being hesitant to commit to the moves you know you need to commit to while you're making your own path is the surest way to let opportunity pass you by.

So why are so many people prone to this kind of hesitance in making decisions? It all starts with our upbringing. From a young age, we're told what we're supposed to do. We're supposed to go to school, get married, get an education, eat our vegetables. What we're "supposed to do" permeates everything about our lives and every phase of our lives. We were raised as "supposed-to people." There's nothing wrong with that, of course, because the people in our lives were instrumental in helping us build our foundation. It's what makes a society strong. But then there comes a time when we must cut the cord and make our own decisions. By this point, we have received the necessary skills from our family, friends, and other acquaintances, and we must take our own steps, make our own path. We need to remove the rose-colored glasses and wake up to reality.

The Wheelbarrow

Ask yourself this question: Why does it feel sometimes like you've fallen into the trap of same old, same old? Why does life sometimes seem boring or bland? It's because, during those stretches, you've been doing entirely too much of what you're "supposed to." You've kept so religiously to the path that your life has gotten bland and predictable. To get away from that feeling, we have to make change. We have to accept that something new and bold has to happen. We need to make a decision: Are people going to manage us, or are we going to manage them?

So how do you do that? You take action. I once heard a story about a man who went to apply for a job at Microsoft back in the days when that company was starting to take off. As it turned out, the man was a qualified candidate for a janitorial position, but when they asked him for his email address so they could contact him, he said, "What's email?" As a result, the man didn't get the job.

Some people might receive news like that—news that they're not good enough to work for the company they're dreaming to work for—and use that as an excuse to curl up for a while, or maybe settle for something that would allow them to fall into that same-old, same-old trap. Not the case for our hero of this story. Our hero, on the day of his rejection from the Microsoft job, decided that he was going to use the resources and knowledge he had at hand to take action.

So he looked and asked around about what his neighborhood needed. He decided in short order that what they needed was fresh produce. He didn't have much money, but he did have the know-how to buy and sell produce, and he did have the money to buy a humble wheelbarrow. So that's what he did every day after that rejection at Microsoft. He always sold the best fruits and vegetables, and his location was perfect. In no time, he was able to upgrade his wheelbarrow to a mobile produce stand. Then, when he had made enough money, he was able to acquire land that allowed him to grow his own produce. Demand was so high that he started hiring people to cart his fresh foods in other neighborhoods, and eventually into other cities. His determination and his take-action mindset took him from one humble wheelbarrow to running a veritable produce empire. He had carved his own path, and his reward was roaring success.

And how did he get there? By focusing on the basics. He knew what he knew, and he knew what he needed to succeed with his simple company. When he was growing that company, he wasn't thinking about marketing plans or killing the competition. He didn't focus on forming a corporate structure. He knew fruit and vegetables, and that's what he sold.

That's not even the best part, either. The best part is that one year he realized that his business had gotten big enough that he needed to hire an accountant. So he called an accountant and asked him when he could bring in his records.

"Just email them to me," the accountant said. "It'll be easier for both of us that way."

And our hero's response? "What's email?"

Ten years after getting rejected by Microsoft for not having an email address, this man still didn't have an email address. He did have millions of dollars, but no way to connect with people online.

"You mean you did all this without knowing what email is?" the accountant asked incredulously. "Imagine where you would've been if you'd only known about this."

Of course the way we all connect with each other almost every day would not have been of any use to our produce seller—and not because of his line of work, either. It's because *action* was the only thing he needed to grow his business. Email can't replace the power of action. Nothing can replace the power of action. Without action, *nothing* is possible. At the end of the day, action cures fear (that last one isn't my quote—it's David J. Schwartz's—but I absolutely believe in it. And I've lived it, too. "I've got to work. I've got to get up and do something." That has been the motivator for every ounce of my success. If I had focused on the stuff I was "supposed to do" like launching a cell phone app or keeping up with my emails, would I be where I am now? Not likely. It was the same story for our produce seller. All those people all around him were doing what they were "supposed to do" for ten years, and he went out, took action, and made a fortune.

Don't Overthink It

For some people, taking action like our produce seller isn't something that comes easily or naturally. After all, if it were as simple as putting your head down and working, everyone would do it. The trouble is that far too many people get caught in the trap of overthinking things. Mulling over your potential actions is important—you've got to stay a course and be logical—but you also have to trust that if you're going to do the right thing and work right and have a singleness of purpose that you focus on, then you need to believe in that journey and the first step you're going to take. Don't think about what might go wrong. Just take that step.

One of the surest and quickest formulas for failure is to overthink things. When you overthink, you talk yourself out of decisions and you create problems that don't exist. This is, in fact, part of why it's so easy to fall into the same old, same old. If you always do what you're "supposed to do," then you never have to think for yourself. If you follow that line of living for long enough, then eventually the idea of trying to think about how you're going to carve your own path gets to be terrifying. That's where faith has to come in (faith in God, faith in yourself, or faith in whatever it takes to get you to make that step). This is true even if you encounter setbacks or obstacles. Those obstacles don't mean you're not doing the right thing. They aren't excuses to start overthinking again. They are opportunities to appreciate how hard you have worked and how much your continued hard work will help you accomplish.

A journey begins with a single step, as they say. More appropriately, think about your idea or your dream not as a journey, but as a balloon. Every bit of action you take is a like a little more air in the balloon that is your dream. But if you stop taking action—if you resort to thinking it through without putting action toward the dream—then you overthink, and overthinking is like a needle. Soon, you'll realize how easy it is to prick all your theories and goals and dreams like they're fragile balloons. So don't overthink it. Accept that your goal has merit, have faith in yourself (or in a higher power), give some thought to it, and then *take action*.

The Path Is Endless

In the previous chapter, I talked about how originality is essential to success. Well, when it comes to taking action and carving your own path, a similar lesson applies. One of the reasons my restaurants have won so many awards over the past fifteen years is because we're different. Equally important, we have stayed relevant all these years because we didn't get comfortable with what we were doing. We never settled for the edge we already had. We kept working toward new things to make us different and to continue evolving.

In earlier chapters, we talked about Polaroid. That company became comfortable and arrogant. Then they got crushed. You've got to be able to distinguish that fine balance between having a great understanding of what you've been doing and getting *complacent*. Think about it this way: The Model T was a tremendous car for its time, but how would it fare on the open roads these days? It may have been the greatest car ever built, but what kind of market would it expect to reach today without air conditioning, power brakes, power windows, power locks, Internet radio, or even windshield wipers? If Ford rolled out a car like that today, it wouldn't sell one unit to anyone outside of a small group of collectors. Ford's modern line of cars, successful as they have been of late, is evidence that you have to grow with your product (or service). Even if you find success early, you can't stand pat and expect to continue that success. The path, in other words, never ends.

That might sound daunting, but it's actually good news. Why would anyone want to sit around and expect their successes to continue without a little effort to keep them fresh? If Yanna and I had stopped working when we received our first award, we would have been out of business by now. Our success has been twenty years in the making. The awards we're getting make it look like it's happening right now, but we put in a lot of time and effort. Along the way, we experienced plenty of times when things didn't look good, and I could have doubted. But imagine if we hadn't introduced vegetarian options or gluten-free or new cooking flares, and so on. That doubt would have derailed us.

Leave Your Comfort Zone Behind

Sometimes moving out of your comfort zone can scare the hell out of you. It's perfectly normal to fear taking a risk. But always remember that the biggest risk you can take is not taking a risk. That doesn't mean to jump into every opportunity without thinking it through. We don't want to follow any knee-jerk reactions here. What I mean is that if you see an opportunity to retool your business and keep your product/service fresh, and you've done your homework, then absolutely you should leave your comfort zone behind.

Here's an example of what I mean: Do you remember life before what has essentially become a nationwide smoking ban in bars and restaurants? Sure, there are still pockets of places where you can smoke indoors, but they get rarer all the time. Back before the ban, I was a smoker myself, so I don't have vivid memories of what an assault on the senses those smoke-heavy rooms tended to be for nonsmokers. But now the ban has been in place for such a long time that most people tell me they can hardly remember what it was like back when smoke hung everywhere. Those that do remember can hardly *believe* they were willing to sit in rooms like that.

The thing is, if you look closely at the period before the smoking ban, many (if not most) restaurants and bars were actively against the ban because they believed it would drive away customers. "Why would I want to narrow my potential customer base?" was the general idea. But my wife Yanna and I didn't see it that way. We believed that inevitably bars and restaurants would have to disallow smoking, and we saw this as an opportunity to get ahead of the curve. Eight years before the smoking ban came to Pennsylvania, we went smoke-free.

Let me tell you, this was especially difficult for me because of being a smoker at the time. But we had a clear personal motivation to go through with it: Yanna and I worked fifteen-hour days, seven days a week, couldn't afford a babysitter (or a state-of-the-art smoke exhaust system for our restaurant), and we wanted to see our son. Our professional motivations were less obvious, but they were absolutely there. It occurred to us that our customers who took great care in their appearance preferred not to go back to work or home with their clothes smelling like smoke. No one likes to have to do laundry just because they sat next to a smoker—and that issue becomes even more compelling when you hold a higher-than-average value on your clothing.

I wish I could say that we dropped the smoking privilege from our restaurant and everything went completely smoothly from the very beginning, but it's not true. As we started telling people about the date that we would stop allowing smoking, our numbers thinned out. Then, the day the new rule went into effect, you could have shot cannonballs through our diner without worrying about hitting anyone. I have to admit, I was so nervous about what we had done that I considered reversing the idea. Yanna and I got close to going back to the norm.

But wouldn't you know it, a friend of mine came in that day and said, "Wow, Billy. What's going on today? I've never seen it so slow in here."

I sighed and told him about how we had decided to go smoke-free. He furrowed his brow. "Is there a new law I don't know about?"

I explained that there wasn't a new law, but that Yanna and I had decided it would be better if we could see our son every day without exposing him to secondhand smoke. "Plus, I had a hunch that people might be attracted to a place that's smoke-free. It's starting to look like I was wrong."

I felt awful having to admit something like that to myself, but as it happened, my friend perked up. He was an anchor on the local news station, and he smelled a story. "Let me do some research," he said. "I think we have a story here. You may be the first place in the area to go smoke-free."

I was hesitant about the story at first, but it worked out extremely well for us. Not forty-five minutes after the story came out, we had an outpouring of support from regular customers, occasional customers, and a huge vote of confidence from people who had never been into the restaurant before. The phone rang off the hook that night and on into the next day, some people pledging support and others promising to come in for a meal. Our weekday business grew to be as strong as what our Saturday business had been in the past. Our weekend business grew into what our holiday business used to be. We were absolutely *booming*. And it kept getting better and better.

There is always great reward for doing the right thing. It isn't simply a moral issue either; doing the right thing tends to generate *excitement*. There's a huge advantage to excitement—not only in the choices you make, but in the way you frame your product or service. Excitement isn't only the most compelling reason to take risks; it's also a tremendous competitive advantage.

In the case of our restaurant, right around the time we went smoke-free, I knew that we had to do something to generate new excitement so we could keep all these new customers. I could have done what many restaurant owners do and purchased some cheesy art and called it a day. That cheeseball effect was all the rage at the time. But instead, I decided to pursue the path that would keep us on the cutting edge. Plasma TVs were still new and expensive enough at the time that few bars and restaurants had them. If I had decided to stay in my comfort zone, I would have seen that as too great an expense to take the risk. But I saw an opportunity. I thought, "Why shouldn't a diner have a big TV showing some headline news with closed captioning while we play some cool European lounge music in the background?" At the time, it might have sounded like a crazy idea, but as far as diners in our area in 2002 were concerned, that was completely cutting edge.

Before we know it, people were calling us the "Hard Rock Café of diners" or "the Cheers of the breakfast world." I wasn't immediately sure whether the changes we made would translate into dollars, but then again, I wasn't chasing dollars. I simply wanted to create a great atmosphere in the kind of place where people don't usually expect anything beyond senior citizen specials and liver and onion plates.

From there, with our smoke-free, technologically forward, and genuinely cool new atmosphere, we saw a vastly different sort of clientele begin to file into our place. The next step was to figure out how to cater to these hipper customers. That's when we began introducing nontraditional and sometimes unusual ingredients to our burgers, omelets, and so on. That was only part of our reasoning. The other part was that Yanna and I couldn't afford to go out to high-end places at the time, so we figured, "You know what? Let's bring this kind of food here. Wouldn't it be great if we could create that high-end experience for people but do it in a diner format?" So we became all about beautiful presentation, offbeat dishes, and good music.

Thanks to those decisions, celebrity has followed. Our restaurant has fed everyone from politicians to musicians to astronauts to boxing champions and everything in between. This came to pass not because of luck, and certainly not because we stayed in our comfort zone. We owe it all to originality. If we had tried to duplicate what the restaurant giants were doing at the time, we'd have no story to tell. Instead, we decided to be different. We decided to make our own path. Our decision to become "not your ordinary diner" took us out of the "supposed-to" category and made us a huge success.

Chapter Seven

Chapter 7 does not belong in this book, and definitely not in your life. So let's skip it and move on to the next one.

Chapter Eight
Just Show Up

"Success is like being pregnant. Everyone says 'congratulations,' but nobody knows how many times you had to get screwed."
—Who cares who said this? It's true.

Here we are in chapter eight of a book about transforming your life, and we're leading it off with one of the most transformative things that can ever happen to a person. First, let me say this: Nothing can or will ever equate to being a mother—and I don't mean to make it sound like success in business and life is an apples-to-apples comparison with pregnancy; I'm only referring to what my wife Yanna has told me. What she told me is that pregnancy and success share a number of similarities. They're both wonderful things that are sometimes difficult to achieve. Plus, along the way, they can both be quite challenging, both emotionally and physically.

Since I'm a man and have no firsthand knowledge of the pain of pregnancy, maybe I should drop the analogy and try to describe the pain in a different way—one to which I can relate. Have you ever seen a movie or TV show or video clip where a person gets kicked in the southern states, and everyone in the theatre cringes? Similarly, transforming your life and your business can be a fragile undertaking. While you're on your path to knowledge and making your ideas a reality, you are vulnerable. Countless ideas have been stolen because of a moment of weakness. Sometimes this is called a breakdown in trust. At its most extreme level, we call it corporate espionage. No matter what you call it, it does happen. And no matter how it happens, there is only one antidote. The one thing you can do to win every day in business and in life, no matter what, is to just show up. It's that simple. Just show up and work. And keep working and don't stop. Even if you're tired, don't stop. Stop only when you're done. That's it.

How do I know this? Well, it all starts with my good fortune to have been able to meet, interview, and feed so many people over the years. I've interviewed everyone from Maria Bartiromo to Harry Connick Jr. to Governor Ed Rendell to Mayor Michael Nutter to the great Tony Orlando to the amazing Criss Angel. I've spoken with musicians, politicians, performers, celebrities, and even to Miss America. In that time, what I've noticed and learned is that even the most successful of these celebrities had one thing in common with the most skilled of entrepreneurs, business owners, contractors, teachers, chefs, and on and on. What is that one thing? They have the same emotions. They all have fear, doubts, and worries, like me or you. The only difference is that the successful refuse to let these feelings stop them.

Get Up and Walk

Sometimes to truly grasp this concept, all we need to do is look at our children. As a father of three great kids, one of my proudest moments was watching my children learn to walk. Any parent can appreciate this. When my kids were learning to walk, they would fall on their ass a hundred times a day. Every time, they would get up and try again. Now imagine how different it would be if, after falling that first time, they had said, "I don't think this walking thing is for me"? If it was in our nature as children to give up the first time we encountered difficulty, none of us would be able to walk—or talk, or feed ourselves, or use the bathroom . . .

You get the idea. So if we're talking success in business and in life, let's take a cue from the toddlers among us. Don't give up. No matter how many times you fall on your ass, all you need to do is get up, show up, and kick ass—it's that simple. It's the surest way of achieving results. Now you need to remember, results usually come in bits and pieces (although there are certainly times when you get the big payoff you've been waiting for). Either way, don't ever take any of your results for granted, especially if they're the big payoffs.

I once asked my dad why he continued to work hard after he achieved true success and the American dream. By that point, he and my mom had no debt. Their business, their home, their cars . . . all paid off. So I asked him what reason he had to continue working so hard, given all that comfort. I can still hear his answer in that broken accent of his. "Number one," he said, "I enjoy what I do. And number two, always remember that success isn't owned; it's leased, and rent is due every single day."

Think about it this way, just because your refrigerator is filled with great food and you had a nice meal today, does that mean you won't be hungry tomorrow? Of course not. You could eat fifteen burgers today and still be hungry tomorrow. Or what if you managed to get ten hours of sleep last night? Does that mean you're not going to sleep tonight? The same applies to the pursuit of success. You don't stop because you're full or you're satisfied. You only stop because you're *done.* The importance of showing up is that you have to do it every single day. Don't do it one day and not the next. Don't do it one day and never again. Don't be a one-hit wonder.

So if you fall on your ass, get up, move forward, and remember that life does not give you what you want; life gives you what you deserve.

You Be You

There is something so important in "you being you." I'm talking here about your own, unique identity, your thoughts and your beliefs merged with the unique challenges that life throws your way on a daily basis. This is where your instincts and originality will come from. The hard work ethic is what will help get you past life's many obstacles. Knowledge must be combined with that hard work ethic. This is part of the formula to you owning you. Showing up leads to hard work, and showing up leads to another critical element that we've discussed already: originality.

Just showing up ensures that no one can steal exactly what you're doing, because nobody can replicate the uniqueness of you. Our restaurants are what they are today because of our originality. Sure, we use a lot of the same ingredients as other restaurants, but we make it in a different, fun, and accessible format that is decidedly and uniquely *us*. Then we throw in some nice conversation at the counter along with the great food, and we're golden. If we'd tried to duplicate what the restaurant giants were doing, we wouldn't be telling this story.

That's the greatest aspect of embracing your uniqueness. First, it gives you an edge over the competition. Second, it ensures that you protect yourself and your business from copycats. Inject a little of yourself into your products, services, or job, and you prevent others from copying them. Second, that uniqueness makes it easier to overcome the challenges and obstacles we discussed at the start of this chapter. Every child struggles to learn to walk. Every child eventually masters it in a unique way. I still laugh when I think about the funny and original little gaits my three children used when they first started walking. Some kids walk like geishas, and others like sumo wrestlers, and you can bet there are a billion variations in between, and each one entirely original. It's the same concept for your uniqueness as a businessperson, service provider, teacher, doctor, you name it. When you do something special, you feel unbeatable. You have an edge, you have an excitement, and you have the ability to climb to any height. It's all that garage start-up concept. Whether you're Apple or Disney or Harley Davidson or some of the greatest bands in the world, you start in that garage, and it's your uniqueness that helps you overcome all those challenges and rise to the top of your industry.

Be Thankful for Who You Are

A great entrepreneur is always thankful for every day he wakes up on this side of the ground. The path to success in any business or profession is the same path to living a fulfilling life. You're going to go through the same steps. Passion, love, understanding, learning, perfecting your craft—all those things will drive you and direct you toward success. If you're driven by finance, that same philosophy will apply. If you want to be an excellent teacher, that applies too. If you want to be a great parent, it's all the same.

You're one of a kind, and if you're an entrepreneur, you understand that fact. You are an individual. There is no one else like you. You're different. Since there is only one of you, you are the only person alive who could offer the world the unique difference you have to offer. So have a good understanding about who you are, don't take anything for granted, and above all, be thankful for that natural edge your uniqueness gives you.

At the end of the day, if you don't have a good, human understanding of who you are, where you live, and why you're important, there's not that much hope for you. So if you have that knowledge, be thankful, because it's going to make you successful in whatever you do.

Put In the Work

Yes, a major component of just showing up is working hard. In an earlier chapter, I mentioned how I used to work so hard that I would deprive myself of sleep as a form of punishment for failing to achieve my daily goals. That is, of course, a crazy thing to do—and I wouldn't recommend it for anyone—but it is illustrative of how serious I am about the importance of hard work. Not sleeping was my way of reinforcing the importance of putting in a good day's work. I only slept if I felt I was worthy of it and if I'd committed properly to my obligations that day. It was by far the dumbest, most ridiculous thing I ever did.

Looking back, though, I realize that it's something I did because I was always pushing myself to be like my hero: my father. Because of how vocal he was about the miracle it is to be able to live and work in this country, I knew that I had to do whatever I could to emulate his work ethic. He explained that I was blessed enough to be born in a country that embraces everything I love: the right to be free, the right to dream, and the right to make those dreams come true. Yes, you do have to make sacrifices to live the quality of life that you want—that's just the way it is—but these are the things we must do as entrepreneurs who strive for success.

Obviously I'm not suggesting that you sacrifice your health, sanity, family, and friends. The message here is that hard work conquers (almost) all. Like anything in life: if you work hard and have a plan, you'll get there. Don't forget about the plan. We can't plug away at something with no direction in mind. For God's sake, just because you like chocolate doesn't mean you should eat a whole box. You have to realize and understand the difference between what feels good and what is right, and the fact is, health and family and good relationships are paramount. If you can't fit these three into your formula, then you will never appreciate success, no matter how hard you work to achieve it.

So that's the final message in our chapter on just showing up. Take those hard first steps. Be yourself. Be thankful for who you are. Work hard. And at the end of the day, make sure to save room for your health and the people you care about. If you can make all of these things happen, then you will have found the ultimate success.

Chapter Nine
WTF

"You can't hit a grand slam if you bunt."
—*Billy Kounoupis*

I have to admit that I agonized quite a bit about this chapter. For one thing, there's the potentially offensive title. But then I decided that I've shared enough colorful language already that what does a little acronym matter? The more important part of my hesitation is that this topic tends to take me to a place I don't necessarily want to go. Still, I think it's important for you to understand that, even with success, you can still be miserable. Why is this? Well, there are many social, financial, and logistical reasons, but the main reason in my view is that the misery comes from that feeling that you still haven't reached your full potential.

The entrepreneurial mindset is tough because it's so driven by the need to *grow* that sometimes it's hard to recognize when the growing is done. Hell, I mentioned in the previous chapter that part of success is never being satisfied that the growing *is* done. Don't eat those fifteen burgers and assume you don't have to eat again tomorrow. The WTF issue here is that it's so difficult to be *thankful* for the process of growing because we're so busy stressing about how we could be better.

I suffered through that for a long time during my journey. It took me years to learn how to let go of the inherent misery of never feeling fully satisfied. In the end, I think what I needed to hear was my dad saying he was proud of me. Obviously I knew that I wasn't going to get that, but now at least I know what I would say if I could hear him speak those words, and that has given me closure and allowed me to concentrate 100% of my focus on what is important in life: happiness—and more specifically, taking the time to enjoy what you *have* achieved, even as you strive to achieve more. At the same time, we can't get so focused on the little achievements that we forget about trying to hit that grand slam. It's a delicate dance but one that anyone is capable of doing.

The WTF Moment

Sometimes life hits you with so many distractions that you forget to focus on a grand slam. I'm not referring to the simple, minor distractions of TV shows or even the media here either. Often, the worst distractions come from the people we love and respect, such as family and friends. Other times, the worst distractions come from people who are just . . . well . . . assholes. The fact is that, no matter where we are in life or where we come from or how far we've progressed in our goals, we all know a few assholes. They're not always outwardly apparent, either. Sometimes their asshole-ness is tougher to spot.

Let me give you an example. As people, we get excited about an idea, concept, or dream. When this happens, the first thing we do is take it to the people we love. Sometimes, when we express our excitement and our brilliance, they give us that "WTF" look. That look can be so crippling. It's not that this person is intending to be mean to you—it's just that sometimes your goal is bigger than what they can even imagine or dream. They come across as an asshole in this situation, even if they didn't intend it.

Let's put something in perspective: Imagine the person who first pitched the idea of sending someone to the moon. Most of the people he told probably looked at him like he had just told him his home planet *was* the moon. Now imagine Neil Armstrong saying to his friends and family, "I'm going to walk on the moon someday." He was probably laughed at more than a few times. Thinking more globally, imagine the Wright brothers telling their friends and family of their intention to build a flying machine. Or if you're not into aeronautics, imagine when Kiss first said, "Hey, you know what might make our band stand out? Putting on tons of makeup and spitting blood on the crowd." In all cases, people probably said, "WTF is wrong with you? Are you on drugs?" That same conversation has happened in every industry from computers to robotics to entertainment, and everything in between. And that conversation will continue to be had for as long as people are willing to dream of hitting that grand slam.

The Bittersweet Moment

I knew that deciding what I wanted to do with my life was going to be a bittersweet moment for me. I understood that my thought process, and the way I saw people, was going to change—especially given that I had made the serious decision that I had a choice to either learn the tricks of the trade or master the trade. When I decided to master my trade, that meant going back to square one and learning the right way to do everything that I'd already been doing for years. When I chose that step, I was able to have a better understanding of my craft because I now knew that there had to be a purpose behind everything I did. If I'd gone along assuming that things had to be done a certain way just because my dad had told me that was the right way to do them, I'd have never reached my full potential.

Even though my life progressed in a positive way, I still had moments of unhappiness and depression. Those moments got to be so frequent that I found myself having to look back at my past so I could try to figure out WTF was going on. Why was it that the success of my restaurants couldn't shake the remainder of my misery? Now that I had acquired a little more knowledge and a newer perspective, I was able to look into my past without fear. My misery and my depression came from not ever being able to let go of my past.

I guess it just took me awhile to accept that I had to let go if I ever wanted to move forward in a way that resembled complete happiness. The truth is I was scared because I didn't want to lose that connection with my father and brother. But after I finally faced that fear and allowed myself to go back to square one—and after spending weeks of talking to myself and crying like a baby and letting my emotions take their course—I eventually ran out of tears. This allowed the confusion to dissipate. Once the cloud lifted, I was able to wash away the misery that poisoned me more than ever before. By looking back, I was able to address and stop fretting about all my failures.

Finally I started to understand that my knowledge and learning my craft was going to provide me with a comfortable future. Fast forward to the here and now, and I now realize that I am blessed. When I walk into my home or my business, and when I am with my family and my friends, I realize now that life is *good* and that God has been great to me. At the end of the day, I realize what my heart and soul needed had exceeded the wants of my eyes. As I looked at the long shadow of success left by my father, I realized that someday I would look him in the eye and say, "I fought as long as I breathed." I finally understood my future. The past was gone, and the future no longer scared me.

Getting There

When I discovered the power of going back to square one, I did so completely by accident. But now that I understand the value of that, I make sure to plan for it on at least a semi-regular basis. Here's why: Each one of my businesses serves around five thousand people per week. I am blessed to be able to write this. I love it, and I am certainly not complaining, but because I'm constantly surrounded by so many people, I can easily get overwhelmed by the crowd. There are times of the day that I need to clear out my cobwebs and try to figure things out and plan the following day. I need time to focus. But as I quickly learned, you can't get organized with a cluttered mind.

At one point I realized that even when I was driving, phone calls, emails, and text messages wouldn't stop. I couldn't wait to find a parking lot to pull into so I could check all the messages. When I would come home, I'd still be writing emails on my phone. It occurred to me that I was wasting my life away by being so connected. I had to make a change for my sanity.

So I started setting goals for myself. I enjoy art, and I've always felt there's no greater artist than God, so I enjoy walking and staring at the beauty He created because it calms my mind. When I'm walking, I have no distractions. I don't talk to anyone. I listen to the music that I enjoy. I do that every day. I also read newspapers every day. I play guitar for thirty minutes every day. I set at least one goal to accomplish around the house, even if it's just to take out the garbage. I try to make it to church. In some form, I need to make sure that I get the two things I need every day: 1) gain some knowledge, and 2) achieve some daily goals. If I do those two things, I'm as happy as I can imagine being.

No matter what goals you set for yourself, it's all about creating a habit and being consistent. My spiritual father, Nicholas Kossis, once said to me during my dark period, "Billy, you are and always will be only one decision away from a totally different life." I asked him to explain to me what he meant, as a priest and a man of faith. I felt that the tone and the context in which he said it was so powerful.

"To lead a good life," he told me, "you must accept what is good, do what is right, and don't ever quit."

These words may seem simple on their surface, but they are absolutely true. For me, no matter how dark things get, as long as I remember these three principles, I know that everything will turn out just fine. You owe it to yourself and to those who support you to accept what is good, do what is right, and never quit.

Chapter Ten
Attempt the Absurd

"Only those that attempt the absurd can achieve the impossible."
—Albert Einstein

When I started putting together my thoughts for this final chapter, I realized that the best thing to do would be to keep it short and sweet. I've shared quite a bit with you in these pages, and now that you've had a chance to absorb it, the most important thing to do is get out there and put it to good use as soon as possible. We've done the reading; now it's time to get to work.

I open with Einstein's quote because it pretty much says it all. Some people think it's impossible to succeed after failing. Some might think it's impossible to succeed without a college education. Some think it's impossible because of their age. I say it's all possible. I truly believe this because I went through it. I failed many times. I don't have a college education. And when I began trying to build my restaurant business, I was at an age when most people didn't believe I'd be able to pull it off. And I'm only one story. The annals of success are full of people who started off with failure, who lacked the prescribed education, and who were supposedly too young or too old to make it in their chosen fields. None of that stuff matters.

What matters is that you make the *attempt*, even if that attempt is, as Einstein put it, absurd.

In the end, it all boils down to this: Just get out there and try.

I have to say that it took quite a bit of trying for me to get to this point in the book. My original goal was to use this process to find peace with myself. But I found that it was tough reliving some of the moments that had so terrified me in the past—moments that made me feel weak and vulnerable. But with every chapter I finished, I started a new chapter in my life. And now that we have bonded with some laughter and tears, I hope that you experience the same thing. I hope that the conclusion of this chapter will open a new chapter in your life. I think my mom put it best in her perfectly broken English when she said, "It's okay to make yourself a priority. There is nothing selfish with doing that. It's just that sometimes it's necessary. You can never forget how much you matter or how much you mean to people, even if you don't see it. I love you."

In the end, I'd like to echo my mother's thoughts here: make yourself a priority. No matter what your doubts about your future or your questions about how you'll make it on your chosen path, you *can* do this. Even if you believe that what you mean to attempt is absurd, as long as you believe it, you *can* make it a reality. It will be a journey, of course, but always remember that the journey will be easier if you get comfortable with being a little uncomfortable. Keep working through the discomfort, and you'll get there. And in the end, you'll have achieved the ultimate goal: that goal to build a life you never need a vacation from. Your success will become your happiness. May God bless your journey.

Acknowledgments

I would like to thank the following people for their inspiration, encouragement, and help with this and other projects:

The city of Bethlehem, the Lehigh Valley, and all of our loyal customers who were with us from the beginning.

The Amazing Crew of Billy's Downtown Diner: You're the best there is; much love to all of you always!

My wife Yanna Kounoupis: You loved me when I didn't love myself, you ignored my failures, you challenged me every step of the way and encouraged me to succeed. You respected me when no one did. You are an amazing mother; you are beautiful and my best friend. As long as I have you, the impossible will always be possible. I love you forever.

My children, the ultimate blessings in my life: Panayioti, Georgia, and Michael Kounoupis, my three amazing kids, you are the highlight of my day, you make me smile when I'm sad, and give me tears of joy. I'm proud to be your dad. I love you more than life. May all your dreams come true and God continue to bless your journey.

My mom, Georgia Kounoupis: God has blessed me with the most amazing mother. You believed in me when I didn't believe in me. My journey would have never been possible without you. I love you.

Father Nicholas Kossis, my spiritual father: Words can't describe how thankful I am for you. Your blessing, prayer, and advice has blessed my journey.

My father-in-law Michael: the best donut maker and awesome Dad .

Dean Tantaros : My best friend and brother, when the world closed the door on me, you and your family opened yours. You are a blessing in my life.

Keith Bachman, CPA: My high school buddy, brother, and amazing numbers guy. If you weren't great at what you do, I couldn't do what I do. Thank you.

Filomena Silvestei: You have been such an amazing blessing to my family and our business. Thank you.

Michael Santanasto Esquire : I am thankful that my friend is also a brilliant attorney who helps me put awesome deals together.

My cousins, Johnny Zannakis, George S. Kounoupis, George C. Kounoupis, Spiro Kounoupis, and my beautiful Cousin Maria Manakos: I think it's safe to say we have been through it all. Our journey together has brought us laughter, joy, tears, anger, and love. We brought the best and worst in each other. With God's blessings may the rest of our journey be a celebration. I love you.

Cousin Christopher Sarantakos aka Criss Angel: You never forgot me, your world class shows, and your creativity has inspired me to do better and never quit. Your filoxinia and friendship has humbled me. I love you and thank you.

Cousin JD Sarantakos: I think the best way to start this is by saying thank you and I love you. Words can't express how much I appreciate all you have done and the projects you have included me in.

To Tony Orlando: Words can't express how much my family and I love you. You are a world-class entertainer, a patriot, and an amazing person. Your songs and presence continue to remind me of precious moments with my dad. I can't thank you enough for being an inspiration, friend, and part of my family and for giving my Michael his first paying job in the entertainment business .We love you.

Cousin Costa Sarantakos: To one of the most honest, smart, and thorough people I know, you probably did not know this, but you have always been the first person to see and read the outlines and transcripts of my books when they were just a thought or an idea. Your honesty and input had a major influence in the direction I would go. Thank you from the bottom of my heart. XO.

John Wilchek Jr.: I can't thank you enough for the support and capturing the amazing photo of the Great Tony Orlando and my cousin JD Sarantakos presenting me with an award for my book

Olaf Starorypinski Photography: Thank you for shooting the cover of my book; you are an amazing talent, and I look forward to working with you again. www.olafstudio.com

Carmen Dancsecs: Thank you for doing my hair and makeup for the cover of my book. It was such a pleasure to work with you, and I can't say enough good things about your work. You are truly an amazing talent.

About the Author

Billy's roots can be traced directly to the influence of his Greek parents Pete and Georgia Kounoupis. They gave up everything in their homeland of Sparta, Greece, to come to America with nothing more than a love of freedom and belief in the entrepreneurial spirit. They taught Billy fundamental values that life is not only about business success but about the importance of dedication to the community. Upon graduation from Easton High School, in the appeal of following in his father's footsteps, Billy's focus was to be a culinary creator like his father. He dropped out of college in his third year and focused on pursuing his entrepreneurial dream. Billy's focus has been to change the standard of the classic American diner to a whole new level. "Not your ordinary diner"™ is his mantra. Gone are the omnipresent stainless steel buildings, the gazillion menu items on oversized menus, and other symbols of an era long past. Billy and his wife Yanna instead focused on creating the Boutique Diners.™ Billy is still active in his restaurants and lectures in schools and universities as well, mentoring and inspiring the next generation of entrepreneurs. His businesses have been mentioned frequently in national and local newspapers and magazines.